Regional Cooperation in South Asia:

A Study on India's Role in SAARC

Regional Cooperation in South Asia:

A Study on India's Role in SAARC

Dr Muzammil Ahad
and
Javid Ahmad Kumar

KALPAZ

First Published, 2018

Published by

Kalpaz Publications
C-30, Satyawati Nagar,
Delhi – 110052
E-mail: kalpaz@hotmail.com
Ph.: 9212142040

Printed at: G. Print Process, Delhi

Cataloging in Publication Data—DK
Courtesy: D.K. Agencies (P) Ltd. <docinfo@dkagencies.com>

Ahad, Muzammil, author.
Regional cooperation in South Asia : a study on India's role in SAARC / Dr. Muzammil Ahad.
pages cm
Includes bibliographical references.
ISBN 9789386397058

1. South Asian cooperation. 2. India—Foreign relations—South Asia. 3. South Asia—Foreign relations—India. 4. South Asian Association for Regional Cooperation. I. Title.

LCC DS341.3.I4A33 2018 | DDC 327.54 23

Contents

Foreword

South Asian Association for Regional Cooperation (SAARC) was established in 1985. It has enlarged its membership from seven to eight (Afghanistan was the eighth member) and nine external and major states joined as observers. India and Pakistan were initially reluctant to join the association due to their apprehensions that both would target each other by associating with neighbouring countries in the region. In order to make these two countries as members, two clauses (no bilateral issues to be discussed and all decision to be taken on the basis of unanimity) were included in the SAARC Charter.

South Asia is viewed as an important region in the world and it is gaining identity across the globe. It is one of the fastest growing economic regions in the world (six per cent growth rate per year). It is trying to integrate with other regions of Asia, which are expected to play a vital role in the global arena. Though there were no significant developments in regional cooperation, the SAARC is the only platform where the member states can debate and discuss various issues related to the region.

On the other hand, there are various factors that prevent regional cooperation in South Asia: suspicion and trust deficiency between India and its neighbours; region was divided by a larger country; bilateral relations dominated and acted as obstacle for regional cooperation; rivalry between two major countries (India and Pakistan); meagre trade among the countries in the region; unable to demarcate their (porous) borders. Conflicts and disputes converted the region backward. There are hardly any pair of states in South Asia, which are not affected by trans-border spilling of ethno-nationalist, communal and militant activity.

Though geographical continuity remains the greatest asset for SAARC, this potential is yet to be harnessed because boundaries have become the manifestation of national identity in the region. Moreover, most of the countries in South Asia are geographically closer to India and unlike the latter no country in the region has geographical proximity with more than two countries. Population and land mass of India are three times greater than the combined of all South Asian countries. And military and economic developments are dominant and make the region as Indo-centric.

India's economic growth is largely driven by domestic factors such as rising consumption and domestic investment, favourable demography, growing affluence and long term encouraging growth prospects. India, despite the low per capita GDP, is a major market. On purchasing power parity basis, India is the fourth largest economy in the world and it is the second fastest growing economy. India's imports have grown rapidly, both in value and share. Thus, India is increasingly being seen as an engine of economic growth in Asia. India, to project itself as a dynamic country, has to play a greater role in bringing stability, peace and security in South Asia.

India was though reluctant to join the SAARC initially, it had played and continue to play a significant role in bringing its neighbours together. Seventy five per cent of regional trade contribute by India. It was reported by ADB that if infrastructure and trade facilities improved trade would be increased from five to twenty four per cent. This can be possible with India's active involvement. Bilateral relations between India and its neighbouring countries will play a major role in enhancing regional cooperation in South Asia.

It gives me great pleasure to write a Foreword to this important and relevant book entitled *Regional Cooperation in South Asia: A Study on India's Role in SAARC* by Dr.Muzammil Ahad, who is known to me as a scholar in the Pondicherry University. I congratulate Dr Ahad for his efforts and dedication to bring out the volume. The volume explains in detail about the factors that made the South Asian countries to realize the importance of regional cooperationand emergence of SAARC as an organization. Further, the volume focuses on India's role in the SAARC in enhancing regional cooperation. The volume certainly contributes and enhances the existing knowledge on the subject. The volume is relevant in the context of India emerging as one of the major economies in the world and South Asia is seen as an important player when power is shifting from West to East.

Adluri Subramanyam Raju,
Director UMISARC
Pondicherry University

Preface

International Relations in the new millennium are gravitating towards a more competitive world order, where the forces of conflict and cooperation are simultaneously at work. While on the one hand, there is a consensus for peace and development, on the other hand, conflicts within and between the states are distributing the international balance. This goal reality is also impinging upon the South Asia.

To minimise the conflicts and work for the peace and development, the latest trend in the world is to link the nations and regions with the rest of the world. This could be seen in the form of establishment of regional organisations throughout the world. Be it European Union, Association of South East Asian Nations, or Arab League, no region or country is either willing or can afford to limit its social, cultural, political or economic activities in the backdrop of globalisation. The emergence of regional organisation and the efforts being made to make them successful has become the order of the day. So accordingly the people of South Asia are also attempting to share their experience in addressing the common problems through one such regional organisation namely, South Asian Association for Regional Cooperation (SAARC).

The idea of South Asian Association for Regional Cooperation was initiated by the late President Zia-ur-Rehman of Bangladesh in 1980 at a time when the South Asian countries were facing many problems like inflation, poverty, income, inequality, large population, malnutrition, diseases, unemployment etc. The countries of South Asia, Afghanistan, Bangladesh, Bhutan, India, Maldives, Nepal, Pakistan and Sri Lanka share many common values rooted in their traditions, which would help as a positive force in generating a climate of harmony conducive to better understanding among the nations of the region.

Since its inception in 1985 and after holding 17 summits and hundreds of meetings at different levels, SAARC has not moved forward in a bid way. The fundamental problem which is mainly responsible for this sorry state of SAARC is the inter-state disputes particularly between its two big members- India and Pakistan. But the keen interest showed by all the members in the recent years' exhibit that there is a lot of scope in its success in the near future. However, the success of SAARC depends on the mutual trust among all the members. It is required that the fear psychosis, suspicion and jealously among the member countries should be removed in order to achieve the desired goal of this organisation.

Abbreviations

AEC	:	Asian Economic Community
AGG	:	Asian Gas Grid
APEC	:	Asian Pacific Economic Cooperation
ARF	:	ASEAN Regional Forum
ASEAN	:	Association of South East Asian Nations
BJP	:	Bharatiya Janta Party
CBM	:	Confidence Building Measures
CENTO	:	Central Treaty Organisation
CSCD	:	Committee on Studies for Cooperation in Development
ECOWAS	:	Economic Community of West Asian States
EEC	:	European Economic Community
EEZ	:	Exclusive Economic Zone
EU	:	European Union
FTA	:	Free Trade Area
GDP	:	Gross Domestic Product
GEM	:	Gender Equality Measures
GNP	:	Gross National Product
GWOT	:	Global War on Terror
HDI	:	Human Development Index
IDSA	:	Institute for Defence Studies and Analysis
IMF	:	International Monetary Fund

ISI	:	Inter Service Intelligence
LTTE	:	Liberation Tigers of Tamil Eelam
NAFTA	:	North American Free Trade Area
NAM	:	Non Alignment Movement
NDA	:	National Democratic Alliance
PTA	:	Preferential Trade Area
SAFTA	:	South Asian Free Trade Area
SAPTA	:	South Asian Preferential Trade Area
SAU	:	South Asian Union
SAVE	:	SAARC Audio Visual Exchange
SDF	:	SAARC Development Fund
SEATO	:	South East Asian Treaty Organisation
SFB	:	SAARC Food Bank

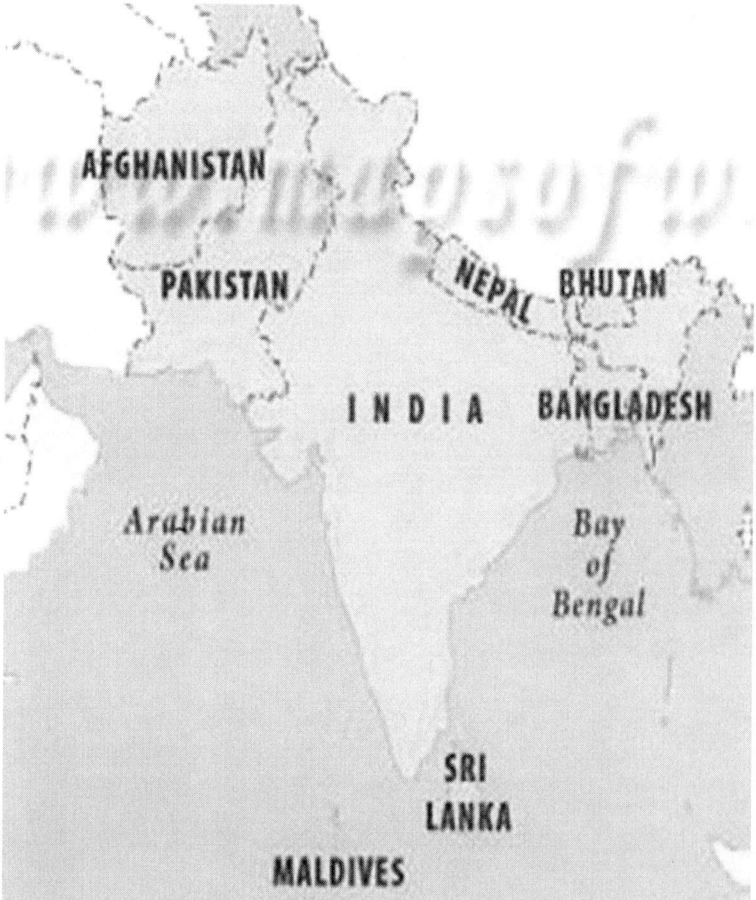
AFGHANISTAN
PAKISTAN
NEPAL
BHUTAN
INDIA
BANGLADESH
Arabian Sea
Bay of Bengal
SRI LANKA
MALDIVES

Map of SAARC

Chapter - 1

SAARC Nations: An Introduction

South Asia as a Region

The traditional literature in international relations particularly the preponderant paradigm like realism envisaged the international system in terms of state centered and conflict oriented anarchical system.[1] The rise of regionalism is analogous to the decline of big power strengths as well as to the eventual emergence of the multi-polarity in international system. Regional integration has been defined as "an association of states based upon location in a given geographical proximity, for the safeguarding or promotion of the participant's interests and an association whose terms are "fixed by a treaty or other arrangements".[2] Regionalism is a preface to achieving order through which universalism can be realised. These regional tendencies have been claimed and supported by functionalism as an arrangement of states as well.[3] Regions in international politics are described as 'a limited number of states linked by a geographical relationship and by a degree of mutual independence' and could be differentiated according to the level and scope of exchange, formal organisations and political interdependence.[4]

The existence of any region can be defined on the basis of presence of certain specific indicators in that area which give it a shape of a region. A set of countries when in close geographical proximity with each other can be said to be categorising a 'region' when; first and foremost they share a certain commonality of national interests. These interests could incorporate a whole gamut of social, economic, political, cultural, historical and other factors; secondly, this set of countries should be sufficiently enlightened so as to understand the significance of placing cooperation above conflict in the conduct of interstate relations.[5] This should also be bolstered by a collective desire to come together on a common plank to create some lashing mechanism for regional cooperation. These sentiments are more or less lacking among the South Asian states, as is evident in years of lack luster performance by the South Asian Association for Regional Cooperation. Following the conception of the SAARC in 1983, very little has been actually done to promote the mechanism for collective cooperation in the subcontinent. There is a lack of cooperation in South Asia in terms of its mutual understanding, political instability and economic cooperation. The main contention is that South Asia is still in the process of evolving as a region due to two basic factors: an adequate degree of complementarities of interests has not yet been achieved among the South Asian States and the almost perpetual preoccupation with intra-state conflicts and crises leaves individual states with scarce time or resources to work towards regional solutions. Such lack of region-ness in South Asia can also be understood in terms of another related phenomenon, that is, the persistence of large number of social, economic and political problems in South Asian Region. Such intra-state problems are often either the cause or consequence of interstate disputes and misperception as well. Thus, there emerges an inextricable connection between the internal and external relations of South Asian states.

Huge size and diversity determines the strength of the Asian region in the world. Its distinct sub-regions–East Asia, Central Asia, South Asia and West Asia–are promising, vibrant and robust. They are critical to the world economy both because of their strategic locations and also the huge commands they have on vital natural resources. There is no uniformity between them in terms of their levels of development. Each region therefore faces diverse challenges.[6] Asia is home to more than 60 per cent of the world population, one-third of the world's economy and largest amount of global foreign direct investment flows into Asia and over a quarter of external exports.[7]

The Asian Continent has become the engine for the revival of the global economy with its large reservoir of entrepreneurial, technical and technological skills and abundant natural resources including oil and gas. Asia is the largest market in the world with an increasing portion of the global workforce and a growing middle class. The rise of China and India has made a profound impact globally in general and in the rest of Asia in particular. China is spearheading changes at a fast pace in East Asia. India's image is growing within its neighbourhood, the Gulf region and to some extent in Central Asia apart from its growing ties with East Asia.[8]

Geography of South Asian Region

Location

South Asia is bounded in the North, North West and North East by the Himalaya's and its sub-regions are marked off from the rest of world by the deep expanses of the Indian Ocean and knit in between the great rivers, systems of the sub-continents landmass. Throughout much of its history South Asia has also been a single entity in some other respects as well.

The South Asian Region dominating the northern half of the Indian Ocean and extending from the Persian Gulf to the Straits of Malacca occupies an important strategic location in an area which has been a hotbed of international politics and conflicts for more than two decades. Geographically, besides the seven countries of the Indian subcontinent with common land frontiers –Afghanistan, Pakistan, India, Bangladesh, Nepal, Bhutan and Burma–the region also includes Sri Lanka and the Maldives islands with common maritime borders with India.[9]

South Asia as a concept is comparatively of recent origin. There is no general agreement with regard to defining the area that constitutes the South Asia. Some would limit it to India, Pakistan, Bangladesh, Sri Lanka, Nepal, Bhutan and Maldives[10], while as others extend it to Afghanistan in the West and Burma in the East.[11] The area possesses geographical contiguity, if Afghanistan and Burma is included and geographical compactness if they are left out.[12] However, both constitute the periphery of the region. In terms of this ethno cultural linkages, Afghanistan is generally accepted as a part of Central Asia and Burma as a part of South East Asia.[13]

The South Asian region is clearly delimited by Iran on the West, from Central Asia and Tibet on the North and from Burma and China on the East. The region is bounded by the Himalayan Mountains on the North, by the Indian Ocean and it's offshoots-the Bay of Bengal and the Arabian Sea on the South, and by mountains and forests on the East.[14] Thus, South Asia's well defined external boundaries provide one of the prerequisites for regional cohesion. South Asia is a sub-region of Asia and covers about 4,48,000 Square Kilometers (1729, 238 sq. miles) or 10 per cent of the continent, and is also known as the Indian Sub-continent.[15]

Sub regions of the South Asia are:

Himalayan States –Northern India, Nepal, Bhutan and Bangladesh

Indian Ocean-Island Nations, Sri Lanka and Maldives Southern–India and Pakistan.[16]

South Asia also provides the context for a wide variety of important political, social and cultural issues. Politically, India and Sri Lanka have established the region's most viable and stable democracies, but even their experiences with democracy has been marked by the occasional lapse into the more authoritarian rule. The other countries of the region have either struggled to institutionalise democracy or even failed to make the effort towards establishing democracy.[17] South Asia is also home to a number of pressing international economic dilemmas. Since independence, the region's states have pursued a wide variety of economic development paths. Some have been relatively successful and others could not sustain the peace of development. Since the end of cold war all of South Asia's major states have embraced ambitious economic liberalisation programmes so as to harness the growth potential of rapid globalisation. As elsewhere, the interaction of domestic economic and global markets has created both winners and losers, along with a backlash that seeks to protect traditional cultures against the potentially homogenising effects of globalisation.[18] While pointing the geo-politics of South Asian countries, it is true that the legacy of state formation in South Asia has been produced almost by a permanent set of relations that pre-empt regional economic cooperation. The political reasons behind this apathy towards regionalisation are well known and involve serious discord in which the countries of the region are entangled. The political tensions and conflicts surrounding the countries of South Asia poses a question of uncertainty and challenge the formation of South Asian Union at par with European Union that allows free movement of people; common currency and common foreign and economic policies which ultimately will sow the seeds of peace and development in the region.

Special geographic features also put one state in a less favourable situation in relation with its neighbour or potential adversaries. A state's dependence on water that originates in another country is one example. The sharing of common water's in South Asia particularly that of Ganges and the Brahmaputra has been the subject of controversial discussion for many years.[19]

History and Culture

South Asia is a realm of one of the oldest civilisations in the world where people from all races and religions have coexisted over a long period of time. The territory of South Asia has been the home of many civilisations both ancient and modern. It is one of the longest civilisations in the world.[20] This layering of different cultures has given it a unique identity that is unparalleled in the world. The people of South Asia speak at least twenty major languages, and if one includes the more important dialects, the count rises to over two hundred. Adherents to every major religion are to be found in the subcontinent. The region of South Asia is a land of diverse, interactive civilisations rooted in their specific linguistic, religious and cultural forms. The South Asian prehistory culminates in the Indus Valley Civilisation, which was followed by the legends of ancient Vedic period and the sketchy references to the rise and fall of Mahajanapadas- the precursors of regional kingdoms and later ancient empires. Almost all South Asian Countries were first under direct or indirect Muslim rule and later under European Colonial subjugation. Much of modern India, Pakistan, Bangladesh and Burma were gradually occupied by Great Britain-starting from 1757, reaching their zenith in 1857 and ruling till 1947. Nepal and Bhutan were to some extent protectorates of Great Britain until after World War II. In the long history of South Asia, this European occupation period is rather short, but its proximity to the present and its lasting impact on the region make it prominent. The network of means of transportation and communication, banking and training of requisite workforce and the existing rail, post, telegraph and education facilities have evolved out of the base established in the colonial era. After World War II, most of the countries of the region gained independence from European colonialism. Since 1947, most of the South Asian countries have achieved tremendous progress in all spheres, particularly education, industry, healthcare, science and information technology, defence related projects, international/global trade and business enterprises and outsourcing of human resources. However, there are still areas which need immediate attention including religious extremism, high levels of corruption, disagreements on political boundaries and inequitable distribution of wealth. The countries of the region share common religions like Hinduism, Islam, Buddhism, Sikhism, Jainism and Christianity. South Asian countries share a common cultural heritage and more or less share same values of life. The whole region celebrates sowing and harvesting festivals almost at the same time. The predominantly agricultural population depends on the monsoon. They dance and joy over its early arrival and pray together when the rain gets late. The wedding season of all South Asian communities comes after the harvest season. The festival 'Vasant' is celebrated with equal gusto in the North India and Pakistani Punjab.[21] Then there is linguistic interlinking in the region. Languages are crossing borders and above all the British rule covered the whole South Asia except Nepal and Bhutan, which were not under direct rule but had a tremendous impact of it. The English language connects the educated elite of South Asia. Hindustani is another means of communication in most parts of the South Asia. The common linguistic populations of India, Bangladesh and Pakistan speak Punjabi and Bengali languages. Tamil connects the Indian state of Tamil Nadu and North of Sri Lanka. Nepali is spoken in the Indian hills of Garwal-Kumau and Darjeeling.[22] It is therefore being realised that by highlighting the cultural forces of unity, increasing people to people contact could be created to ease the tension in the region.

South Asia: A Survey of Basic Data

The basic problems of all the countries of South Asia are similar in nature although with small differences. In varying degrees, all of them are underdeveloped, having large masses of their population on the margins of subsistence and engaged with agriculture. These states have failed to keep pace with the increasing expectations of the people and are not in a position to run and progress according to the dynamic and regular fluctuations in the market. They have not been able to speed up according to the demand-supply curve which is needed to sustain a development over a large period of time. The political systems of these countries are not functioning according to the demands of the times. Governance remains a huge challenge across the region. Public trust in the ability of politicians and governments to deliver growth and justice is decreasing. This often raises the issue of legitimacy of the governments to govern. It is in this context that a commission in India was formed under the Chairmanship of M.N. Venkatachalia in 2000 by NDA government (National Democratic Alliance) to review provisions of the constitution so as to make constitution relevant to the present times. These countries still cling to their colonial legacy. Most of the political systems have hereditary and dynastic character. All of them are in need of radical, structural and institutional changes and have a long way to go before their administration and political institutions will fulfill the needs of their people.

Though the governments of India, Pakistan, Bangladesh, Sri Lanka and Nepal have been making efforts to improve their socio-economic conditions through democratic means there attempts have been frustrated by the background of colonial rule and society's behest by extra-ordinary religious, ethnic, and linguistic complexity. Among the issues related to welfare, the most important concerns of South Asia include limiting population growth, raising literacy levels especially poverty, and addressing environmental degradation. South Asia today contains 21 per cent of the world's population. At present levels of growth, the most recent World Bank projections for the year 2025 put India's population at 1.3 billion, Pakistan at 244 million, Bangladeshi at 180 million, Nepalese at 38 million, and Sri Lanka at 24 million.[23] These high rates of population growth threaten to undermine the benefits of economic development, as well as advances in agricultural productivity, and place massive pressures on the land and its resources. With a substantial population living below poverty line in most of the

South Asian countries (one–third, in the case of India) and with extremely low physical quality of life indices (39 for a well-established democracy like India), none of these nations can really afford to add detriments to their overall growth and progress. In fact, the South Asian Region contains more people living in abject poverty than any other region of the world. In terms of providing for these people, the nations of the region are required "to run in order to stand still".

Economic Growth

South Asia has the highest incidence of poverty not only in terms of absolute numbers but also as a percentage of the population, compared to any other regional group of countries in the world. All the countries of the South Asian region are facing common issues like poverty, income inequality, low productivity, mass unemployment and large population dependent on agriculture. Poverty has been the main handicap in the smooth progress and development of South Asia. About 29 per cent of India's, 33 per cent of Pakistan's, 42 per cent of Nepal's and 50 per cent of Bangladeshi's still live below poverty line.[24] South Asia has been the fastest growing region since the 1990's. Investment as a percentage of GDP has also been consistently on the rise since the 1960's. Productivity in some parts of the region (such as India and Pakistan is at par with China, Thailand and South Korea). However, poverty has not declined much. China and Indonesia managed to halve poverty during the same period. At the same time service delivery in both health and education has remained weak. South Asia is spending less than sub-Saharan in both the cases. Most of the poor people of the region lack effective property rights. Poor people, in particular women and children suffer from unsafe working conditions because their employees operate outside the formal legal system. They are often denied economic opportunities as their property and business are not legally recognised. They cannot access credit or investment, neither can operate within global or local markets. Another important issue is income inequality which has handicapped the smooth growth in the region. The region is very poor in terms of natural resources although rich in respect of Himalayan and maritime potential.[25] South Asia is among the least developed regions in the world as far as its economic parameters are concerned.

The countries of the region have wide differences in the level of their economies. The Per Capita GNP in the region ranges from US $180 in Nepal to US $1000 in Maldives. Industrial production accounts for about one-fourth of the gross domestic product and provides employment to less than 15 per cent of the total population of this region. The position of their balance of trade and terms of trade follows unfavourable trend.[26]

Agriculture

The major portion of the South Asian population is directly or indirectly related to agriculture. Besides, agriculture is contributing most to the country's GDP (Gross Domestic Product) along with the service sector. The growth rate of agriculture is less than the growth rate of population in some countries of the sub-continent. Only India and Sri Lanka and to some extent Pakistan are self-sufficient in food grain production. The unequal distribution of land often leads to the stagnation of agriculture and rural poverty in the concerned countries. This results in a relatively small number of landlords holding large and an overwhelmingly majority with small land holdings. This increases the gap between rich and poor in the region. The ever increasing population in case of South Asia has often led to the narrowing down of land holdings and thus reduced the productivity factor. Land reforms which could have reduced these inequalities have not been effectively carried out in the region.[27]

Population and Manpower

South Asia ranks among the world's most densely populated regions with 1.5 billion people. Among which about one-third of all Asia's population and about one-fifth of the world's population are concentrated in South Asia. The population density of the region is 309 persons per sq. km which is more than seven times the world average.[28]Although the region is rich in terms of human population but when it comes to productive population there is a lot of difference. The continent has become the engine for the revival of the global economy with its large reservoir of entrepreneurial, technical and technological skills and abundant natural resources including oil and gas. Asia is the largest market in the world with an increasing portion of the global workforce and a growing middle class. It had a labour force of 298 million in 1995, which was showing an annual growth rate exceeding two per cent. In the present era of information technology this manpower, if given proper direction would be of immense helpful to the region as a whole. There is a need for providing job opportunities to the growing work force in the future developmental strategies of the states of the South Asian region.[29]

Health and Education

In South Asian Region the health conditions show a remarkable improvement from the last several decades, yet the public expenditure on this sector is very small and needs more attention. There is no formal policy to mention how much and in what way the amount should be spend on health facilities. After more than 60 years of independence, millions of people are without elementary health facilities, safe drinking water and no access to basic sanitation facilities. A lot of migration from rural to urban areas is experienced due to the lack of health and other facilities in rural areas in South Asia. Moreover South Asian Region is mostly rural in character however the growth rate of urban population is alarmingly high exceeding four per cent in Pakistan, Bangladesh, Nepal and Bhutan. The high urbanisation exacerbates environmental problems and creates opportunities for socio-political unrest.[30]

Despite some improvements in the past decades, the literacy rates remained disappointingly low throughout the South Asia, particularly in rural areas. This high illiteracy rate weakens the family planning efforts, limit farmer's abilities to utilise technological improvements, and produce labour efficiency in the general manufacturing sector. The adult literacy rate (57.6 per cent) of the region is lowest in the world.[31] The South Asia is still lagging in literacy chart and is figuring very low as compared to developed countries which are about to touch the three figure mark in literacy rate.

There are more children out of school in South Asia than in rest of the world, and two third of this wasted generation is female. According to a recent U-NICEF[32] study, the worst affected region for malnourished children is South Asia and half of the children in

South Asia are underweight, despite the much higher GNP growth rate and a more robust increase in food production in South Asia. Furthermore, South Asia's gender equality measure (GEM), prepared by the United Nations Development Programme (UNDP) reports that economic and political opportunities open to women are lowest as and it shows the lowest value (0.235) among all the regions in the world. South Asia is the region that defies the global biological norm with only 94 women for every 100 men (instead of 106 women to 100 men in the rest of the world), so that 74 million are simply missing. This shows the negative trend of sex ratio of South Asia. The extent of human deprivation in South Asia is also colossal. About 260 million people lack access to even rudimentary health facilities not to speak of proper health facilities, 337 million lack safe drinking water accesses, 830 million have no access to basic sanitation facilities and over 400 million go hungry each day. This adds to the already ugly picture of South Asia in the world.

Environmental Degradation

Environmental degradation in South Asia is analogous to the region's population problem apart from having several negative socio-economic and politico-security implications. The dependence of the poor regions of South Asia on natural resource base, such as soil, water, forests and fisheries is self-evident but environmental abuse is rampant to an unbelievable degree. Deforestation (particularly in Sri Lanka and Nepal), soil erosion, droughts (in Bangladesh and certain parts of India), floods (frequently experienced in Bangladesh due to situation of rivers and channels) are some of the environmental problems confronting South Asia. As per statistics, the region is also losing a considerable amount of productive land due to a water logging and salinity. In India alone, over three million hectares are believed to be affected by salinity and up to 8.5 million hectares by water logging. Nearly five million acres of forests are cut down each year in South Asia, with only feeble efforts at reforestation. Water, especially river water generated by the rain cycle is the largest resource of the region, especially when considered in conjunction with the population. But as believed by many experts, the highest constraint on the future growth of the world's economy is going to be shortage of water. Fresh water resources are getting depleted at rapid speed, due to the increasing environmental degradation. Moreover, such problems also have spill over ramifications for the region (like aggravating global warming and depletion of the ozone layer). Most of these environmental problems, finally, link up with the desperate poverty of people in South Asia; for want of any viable alternatives for sustaining their livelihoods, they have no choice but to denude and destroy the very land, forests, and water resources.

Role of Religion

There is no better laboratory in the world than South Asia for anthropologists to study religion. South Asia provides platform for almost all the major religions of the world. Many of these religions cut across the national boundaries, which affect the shaping of foreign policies of the respective states.[33] Over the years the region has witnessed the phenomenon of religious revivalism. The political mobilisation for electoral gains has also sharpened religious differences. In order to gain votes the political parties have exploited the religious sentiments. There have been religious based political parties working in South Asia for decades now. They have even been elected to power in some states of South Asia. In India, we have a number of parties that owe their origin to religion. In Bangladesh and Maldives, there are religious based political parties. Even during campaigning of elections religion is used as a tool to exploit the people's sentiments. Since elections are fought on religious lines, South Asian societies are witnessing religious divisions. After the division of sub-continent along communal lines, religion has become a primary factor contributing to the growth of extremism and numerous other forms of political and sectarian violence in South Asia.[34] The destruction of the controversial Babri Mosque at Ayodhya in December 1992 symbolised the communal frenzy which gripped the region in the late twentieth century. The religion extremism nexus often shows itself in places of worship being utilised for terrorist activities. The Sikh insurgency in Punjab reached its climax in 1984 when Akali militants led by Jarnail Singh Bhindranwale took refuge in the sacred Golden Temple in Amritsar.

Developmental Considerations

Development has been an attractive and powerful idea. It has dominated the political landscape of countries in the South ever since their decolonisation mostly after the Second World War. Notwithstanding criticisms and condemnations it continues to be an important component of state policy in most of these countries. The seven nations of South Asian region, commonly suffer from problems pertaining to agriculture, water, power, environment and healthcare. The region shares common agricultural problems concerning of availability of high yielding varieties of seed, manure and pesticides. Problem of water and power remains a common issue among farmers of the region. The region has been the victim of poverty, hunger, malnutrition, population explosion etc. Some parts suffer from the problem of plenty other areas faces starvation deaths. Water problems have been a serious issue between India and Nepal and India and Bangladesh. The Indus Water Treaty is similarly the question of serious issue between India and Pakistan signed in 1960 under the auspices of the World Bank.[35]

Terrorism and Security Environment

Political violence and the use of terror are as old as human history. There is hardly a day without terror attacks in one or the other parts of South Asia. South Asia is the second most violent place on earth after Iraq. Conflicts in Afghanistan and Pakistan have attracted global attention. Parts of India, Sri Lanka, and Nepal are experiencing long-running conflict. Terrorism is a problem South Asia is facing for more than three decades. Today, terrorism is perceived as a major threat capable of destabilising not only national but also international peace. The menace of terrorism has not only affected the developing countries but developed countries as well. South Asian nations, particularly India, Sri Lanka, Pakistan and Afghanistan are victims of menace of terrorism. Indian states such as Punjab, Kashmir and North Eastern states are engulfed by anti-state elements. Conflicts result in death, misery, social trauma, destruction of infrastructure and have huge spillover effects.

Former American President Bill Clinton described South Asia as the "most dangerous place on the surface of the earth".[36] South Asia is one of the most militarised regions in the world. The wide spread human deprivation contrasts sharply with large armies, modern weapons and expanding military budgets. Indeed two of the largest ten armies in the world are in South Asia and it is also the only region where military spending (as a proportion of GNP) has gone up by 12 per cent since 1987, while it declined substantially in all other parts of the world after the end of the cold war.[37] The insecurity scenario is conspicuously reflected in the defence expenditure of all the seven nations of the South Asian region. About 40 million US dollars are spent by Nepal on its security, Bangladesh spends 400 million dollars, Sri Lanka 500 million $s, Pakistan 4.5 billion $s and India spends 7.5 billion US $s. This type of mad arms race has cost a great threat to the regional security. This growing trend of enhanced defence spending by all South Asian nations has raised the security concern of the region. Sri Lanka, Nepal and Bangladesh are looking beyond South Asia to keep themselves militarily secure. India also had complains against Myanmar, Bhutan, Nepal and Bangladesh for allowing the terrorist organsations of North Eastern India to utilise their territories to run terrorist camps. Sri Lanka, on the other hand, had problems with India helping Tamil terrorist organisations form Sri Lanka.[38] The most redeeming feature is that China has become Islamabad, Dhaka and Colombo's main supplier of arms. However, there are some people who believe that the nuclear deterrence has been helpful in establishing long term peace.[39]

Inter-State Conflicts

South Asia is one of the critical regions with complex security in the world, primarily due to the fact that most of the South Asia is engulfed with varying degrees of conflicts and disputes. The main reason for the permanent nature of these conflicts is the demarcation of boundary by the colonial masters in a rugged manner. There are conflicts because of commonalities in certain aspects prevailing in South Asia. Interstate conflicts in South Asia probably are highest compared to any other regional block. Bilateral relations are defined by antagonism and mistrust. The differences between India and Pakistan over Kashmir, between Sri Lanka and India over the nationalities of Tamils, between Nepal and India on open borders and the Indo-Nepal treaty of peace and friendship of July 1950 AD.[40]

India has dispute with almost all states of South Asia. There is a sort of mutual distrust among all the members of SAARC. The most important and critical issue of the world is in South Asia, that is Kashmir issue between India and Pakistan. The origins of Indo-Pakistan conflict have been traced to many sources, the failure of the British to manage a peaceful and politically acceptable partition, the deeply rooted political rivalries between the subcontinent's major religious communities-Hindus, Sikhs and Muslims; the struggle for control over Kashmir; Kashmir's importance to the national identities of both states, and the greed or personal short sightedness of leaders on both sides of the border, in particular, Nehru's romance with Kashmir and his Brahamanical arrogance (Pakistani interpretation) or Mohammad Ali Jinnah's vanity, shortsightedness and religious zeal (Indian interpretation).[41] The two countries, India and Pakistan, have fought almost three wars over Jammu and Kashmir. Relations between India and Sri Lanka have been soaring because of the Tamilian issue. The ethnic crises which prevailed for long deeply affected their bilateral relations wherein India's asymmetry factor loomed so large that Sri Lanka felt compelled to seek extra-regional linkages to offset Indian dominance.[42] The peace accord of 1987 was resented by many on both sides of the divide and some another even commented," by one stroke of pen as it were, Sri Lanka was brought in to India's security fold under its terms.[43] With the withdrawal of Indian peace keeping force (IPKF) from Sri Lanka and assassination of Rajiv Gandhi by the LTTE forces in 1991 compelled India to adopt a hands-off policy and term the ethnic crises as an international issue of Sri Lanka. Actually they were the plantation labourers who were taken by colonial rulers of Great Britain to this island country of Sri Lanka as an indenture labour during colonial regime. There have been disputes between India and Bangladesh over illegal migration of the people from the Chittagong hill tracks (CHT) and the demarcation of boundaries involving fertile islands and enclaves and also in sharing the water of river Ganga.

All these accusations are not unfounded. There exists a defined motive by the countries in the region to extend its shape of influences and weaken their neighbours. This phenomenon is leading to interstate conflict and proxy war.[44]

Intra-State Conflicts

South Asia's ethnic demography provides a fertile arena for several cross border conflicts. It might be more useful to imagine South Asia not as a sub-continent of separate sovereign states but as one of graded ethnic differences.

South Asia provides a disappointing picture in social, economic and political context due to the fact that it is almost perpetually plagued by various intra-state conflicts which are based on divisive considerations of caste, religion, ethnicity, language, community and the likes. This distorts the national identity and the overall order and situation of the affected areas.[45] South Asia has also witnessed a number of deadly ethnic conflicts. In addition to Kashmir, these include counterinsurgency in the far North East of the country, Afghanistan's internecine civil war; Pakistan's struggle to contain civil unrest in Karachi's ethnic cauldron, Bangladesh's Chittagong Hill Tracts violence and Sri Lanka Tamil insurgency. Most of South Asia's ethnic conflicts have international causes and effects, owing to the post-colonial phenomenon of distinct ethnic groups being artificially divided by international borders. Similarly, the regions uneasy mix of religion and politics has important international dimension. For example, no account of Indo-Pakistan relations can afford to ignore the domestic political influence of Pakistan's radical Islamists and India's Hindu right extremist. The problem of civil violence in recent years has emerged as a more serious issue than the problem of interstate warfare in South Asia. After partition Jawaharlal Nehru, the first Prime Minster of independent India said that the greatest threat to India is not from outside, but this is within in the form of diverse caste, language, religion etc. Corruption is another menace that has surrounded every state in its own way. Similarly lot of corruption has been witnessed almost from all South Asian countries' in one form or the other. The recent evidences of corruption in India highlight this point, where high officials and ministers are involved in corruption. The Indian state has been variously preoccupied with separatists and religious conflicts such as in the state of Punjab and Jammu and Kashmir-for the separatists, Mizoram, Assam and Nagaland (North East India)-for autonomy and in Gujarat, Mumbai and other parts have certain religious, ethnic and psychological underpinnings.[46]

Other South Asian countries are facing the same kind of problems such as, the Maoists movement in Nepal, Tamil-Sinhalese ethnic conflict in Sri Lanka which has now turned into a civil war in that country. Although the civil war in Sri Lanka has come to an end, but the case is that until and unless Sri Lankan government will come to accept the genuine demands of Tamils barring claim for separate statehood, the prospect of Sri Lanka seems to be dark. In Pakistan, the society at large is gripped in violence derived from ethnic, sectarian and religious differences.

Similarly, Bhutan and Maldives- the two smallest members of the SAARC also have their own internal problems. The emerging internal problems in Bhutan and the fall out of attempted coup in Maldives in 1987 have varying affects in uniting the country for the cause of development. All this can largely be attributed to the fact that politically governing institutions in most of the South Asian countries are weak. Taken individually each of the South Asian states suffer from some kind of instability and consequently projects varying intensities of human deprivation.[47]

Indo-Centric Region

South Asia is a region marked with serious imbalances in essential attributes of the states i.e. territory, population and natural resources. From this perspective India always predominates in South Asia. India contains nearly 76 per cent area of total region, its population is three times more than the combined population of other six countries of the region and its GNP is 71 per cent of the total GNP in the region. Geography has provided India a central position in the region.[48] It shares borders (land or sea) with all the countries of the region. No other country of the region shares borders with other country except India. This Indo-Centric nature of the region has been the major source of dissonance. The Indo-Centricity along with asymmetry in size, resources and capabilities has given a feeling of insecurity among all the smaller states of the region. They feel over shadowed by India, and this perception often gets strengthened by India's tendency of behaving like a 'Big Brother'.

Viewed from either the global or regional perspective, South Asia provides a disappointed picture in social, economic and political context. South Asia accounts for 21 per cent of the world population and 3.5 per cent of the total land area, but the share of South Asia in world output is merely1.3 per cent. About half of the world's poor are found in South Asian countries. Their per capita GNP ranges from US 180 $s in (Nepal) to US 1000 $s in (Maldives).The average per capita GNP of these countries is barely US 350 $s. The economic structure of these countries is basically agrarian. About three-fourth of their population subsists on agriculture. The imports of the SAARC countries are mainly composed of manufactured goods from the developed countries.[49]

South Asia is viewed as a region of protracted animosity. It is a land of linguistic and cultural diversity. Various ethno-political and religious conflicts have transformed it into a potential threat not only to regional peace but also for global peace and security. The 1998 nuclear tests by two super-powers of SAARC, the Kargil crisis of 1999, the Parliament attack of 2001, continuing unrest in Sri-Lanka and Nepal, attacks on Mumbai in November 2008 made the world community concerned about the future of this region in the age of globalisation and mutual interdependence. Kofi Annan, former Secretary General of the United Nations visited South Asia in March 2001 and depicted the socio-economic conditions of South Asia in the following words 'the fact is that South Asia which is the most heavily populated region in the world faces more daunting problems than any other part of the globe. It has the most appalling poverty, illiteracy, malnutrition and human deprivation than anywhere else in the world'. As long as governments continue to focus on their conflicts with their adversaries and seek a military solution to their disputes, there is no possibility of bringing progress, development and prosperity to their people.

The world development report 2000-2001 of the World Bank acknowledges that while social indicators such as fertility, mortality and life expectancy rate in developing countries have improved on an average basis in the past decades; poverty in the developing world has been shifting towards South Asia and Sub-Saharan Africa. The hope emanates from tremendous human and natural resource potential and richness and variety of its civilisation. The fear arises from the fact that South Asia is not only the poorest region in the world, but also one where the probability of an accidental nuclear war is perhaps greater than in any other part of the world.[50]

Broad improvements in human welfare will not occur unless the downtrodden and poor people receive wider access to affordable and better services in health, education, water supply, sanitation and electricity. Freedom from illness and illiteracy cannot be achieved by the poor unless these services are provided by the respective governments.[51] South Asia despite being the poorest region is at the same time, the most militarised region in the world. The arms race between India and Pakistan, the two countries accounting for 93 per cent of the total military expenditure in South Asia is primarily responsible for this cruel irony. Nobel laureate Amartya Sen slammed India's defence budget for harming the countries human development programme. The military expenditure is being very high and affects key areas like healthcare and education, which requires massive investment.[52] According to Mahbob Ul Haq Human Development Center report on human development in South Asia, India was ranked by the World Bank at 142nd in terms of per capita income and first in terms of arms imports; Pakistan is not far behind, being ranked 119th in terms of per capita and 10th in world in terms of arms imports. What is even more significant is that, while global military spending declined by 37 per cent during the period of 1987-1994, military spending in South Asia increased by 12 per cent. According to the Human Development Report 2002 published by UNDP, Pakistan spends 4.5 per cent of its GDP on defence while India spends 3.0 per cent. On education, Pakistan allocates 2.7 per cent of GDP and India allocates 3.2.[53]

This military expenditure, whose scale is unprecedented in the Developing World, is being done in the name of national security. In this respect human security needs have been ignored which is clear from the fact that Pakistan spends 0.7 per cent of its GDP and India spends 0.8 per cent only on health sector.[54]

In a region where 22 per cent of the entire population or 276 million people have no access to basic health facilities, 540 million people or 35 per cent of the population are living with daily incomes of less than one dollar, 11 per cent of population or 278 million people have no access to safe drinking water, 63 per cent population is without access to sanitation, 45.5 per cent of the adult population is illiterate and 47 per cent of the children are malnourished.[55]

Table I: SAARC Countries: Human Development Index

Countries	*1990*	*1995*	*2000*	*2001*	*2010*	*2011*
South Asia	NA	NA	NA	NA	0.518	0.548
Afghanistan	NA	NA	NA	NA	0.349	0.398
Bangladesh	0.414	0.443	0.478	0.502	.469	0.500
Bhutan	NA	NA	0.478	0.502	NA	.522
India	0.519	0.553	0.577	0.590	0.519	0.547
Maldives	NA	NA	0.743	0.51	NA	NA
Nepal	0.413	0.451	0.490	0.499	0.428	0.458
Pakistan	0.440	0.472	0.499	0.499	0.490	0.504
Sri Lanka	NA	NA	NA	NA	0.658	0.691

Source: Human Development Reports of UNDP.

According to a 2005 report of the human development centre, South Asia is fast emerging as the poorest, most illiterate, most malnourished, least gender sensitive-indeed, the most deprived region in the world today. The per capita gross national product (GNP) of South Asia ($ US 309 in 1993) is lower than any other region in the world. The region contains 21 per cent of the world's population but produces only 1.3 per cent of the world's income. The adult literacy rate (48 per cent) in South Asia is now the lowest in the world. The migration of the landless into cities exacerbates urban environmental problems and creates opportunities for socio-political unrest. Moreover, the movement of the people across the subcontinents borders in search of food and employment causes friction within and between the regional neighbours. Further, despite some improvements in the past four decades, the literacy rates remain disappointingly low throughout the region, especially for females and in the rural areas, the overall adult literacy rate for India is an estimated 48 per cent, for Pakistan and Bangladesh about 35 per cent and for Nepal 26 per cent. High literacy rates stifle family-planning efforts, limit farmers abilities to neutralise technological improvements and reduce labour efficiency in the general manufacturing sector, Sri Lanka has achieved solid success in improving literacy rate which is close to 90 per cent. Although most of the South Asian countries have recently initiated varying degrees of economic reforms by adopting liberalisation and free market economic policies, the persuasive and innate character of their domestic/regional problems tends to negate most of the constructive efforts. In view of the fact that South Asia imported 18 per cent of total arms produced in the world, the logic of such large and growing military expenditure needs to be questioned. The tradeoffs between military expenditures and the provisions of basic services are worth considering. According to Mahbob-Ul-Haq, a battle tank normally costs 4 million dollars, immunizing a child against deadly diseases costs one dollar. For the purchase of each battle tank, four million children could be immunised. A mirage (war plane) reportedly costs 90 million dollars. It costs an average of 30 $s to maintain a child in primary school. Three million children can be benefitted against the same amount and be provided primary school education. Against the purchase of three Agosta 90B submarines, 17 million children could have been provided with primary schooling, while 67 million couples could have been facilitated with family planning services.[56] The question arises whether national security can be sustainable when achieved at a heavy cost to the citizen's health, education and wellbeing. Income disparities in South Asia are one of the biggest in the world. All the countries of the region have a dramatic concentration of wealth and power.

The inability of South Asia to execute its determination for progress is reinforced in its performance towards achieving millennium development goals (MDGs). According to Asia's regional press release by the United Nations[57], with the exception of Southern sub-region, Asia is going well towards realising the MDGs. Afghanistan's 2012 HDI of 0.374 is below the average of 0.466 for countries in the low human development group and below the average of 0.558 for countries in South Asia. From South Asia, countries which are close to Afghanistan in 2012 HDI rank and population size are Nepal and Pakistan, which have HDIs ranked 157 and 146 respectively.[58]

Table II: Afghanistan's HDI indicators for 2012 relative to selected countries and groups

Country	*HDI Value*	*HDI rank*	*Life expectancy at birth*	*Expected years of schooling*	*Mean years of schooling*	*GNI per capita (PPP US$)*
Afghanistan	0.373	175	49.1	8.1	3.1	1000
Nepal	0.463	15	69.1	8.9	3.2	1137
Pakistan	0.515	146	65.7	7.3	4.9	2556
South Asia	0.588	NA	66.2	10.7	4.2	3343
Low HDI	0.466	NA	59.1	8.5	4.2	1633

Source:- Human Development Report, 2012.

The child birth rate in South Asia is 480 per 10,00,000 births in the region. Part of this toll can be attributed to the poor health of mothers. About 85 per cent of the pregnant women aged between15-49 is suffering from anemia. Many of the children, who survive birth, do not live beyond infancy. Infant mortality rate per 1000 live births in the entire region is 75.[59]

Throughout the South Asian region there are only 44.34 doctors per 1,00,000 people. One nurse for every 4078 people but by contrast there is one policeman for every 939 people. Thus, there are a four times as many policemen as nurses or doctors. The region has the teacher student ratio of 1: 60.[60]

Declining education levels and adverse living conditions push people into worst living conditions i.e., desperation and prostitution and anti-social activities. Child prostitution is widespread, poverty and inadequate social safety nets have left many children with no choice but to sell parts of their bodies simply to survive from one day to the next.[61] Furthermore, the heavy arms buildup and constant conflict in South Asian countries have taken their toll in the guise of subverting the basic social fabric of society. Be it Pakistan, India, Nepal or a Sri Lanka, they all have become highly militarised, bigoted and intolerant nations. They believe that a change from a belligerent to a peaceful foreign policy based on the principle of co-existence would jeopardize the existence of all South Asian countries.[62]

Table III: Regional performance of SAARC Countries

Indicators↓ /Country→	*Afghanistan*	*Bangladesh*	*Bhutan*	*India*	*Maldives*	*Nepal*	*Pakistan*	*Sri Lanka*
Area 'sq.km'	647500	147570	38394	3287263	298	147181	796,095	65610
Coastline (Kms)		580		7,516			1,046	1,340
Population (2011) million	28,395,716	142,310,000	708427	1,210,193,422	3,13,920	2,66,20,000	17,71,63,231	2,06,53,000
Population ensity (sq km)		1,074	18	366	1,037	199	215	308
Life expectancy years		63	64	63	67	62	65	74
Literacy rate		38.1	42	65.38	93	35.7	42.2	89.3
Growth rate (per capita GDP (% per year) 2011	3.7	5.4	6.3	5.5	5.7	1.3	0.3	7.2
GDP ppp ($ billions) 2010	27.433	258.608	3.875	4,057 trillion	2031	35.813	482.913	106.5
GDP (PPP) ($ per capita 2010	909	1,572	5,429	3,408	9005	1270	2851	5220
GDP (nominal) ($ billions)	15541	104.919	1.412	1.631 trillion	2.062	15.836	202.831	49.68
GDP (nominal) ($ per capita)	515	638	1,978	1,370	6,336	562	1,197	2435
Per capita foreign exchange		14.5	80.7	23.9	243.7	27.1	6.1	118.2

(Contd...)

Gross national income per capita ($ billions)		440		620		250	600	1,010
Military expenditure (% of GDP)		1		2	8	2	4	3.
Purchasing power arity ($ billions)		274		3369		39	330	82
Currency	Afghani	Taka	Ngultrum	Rupee	Rufiyaa	Rupee	Rupee	Rupee

Source: Asian Development Bank Report, 2012.[63]

From the Table III, it is clear that India has the largest area, coastline, population and GDP among the SAARC countries, whereas Maldives has the smallest area, least population and GDP. However, the annual growth rate of population was as high as 3 per cent in Maldives and as low as 1.4 per cent in Sri Lanka. Further in case of Sri Lanka, life expectancy and literacy rate were also highest, i.e. 72 years and 89.3 per cent respectively, which were, lowest, i.e., 49 years and 2 per cent respectively in case of Bhutan. While Pakistan has 33 per cent urban population, Bhutan accounted only 6 per cent for the same. The per capita GDP in terms of purchasing power parity of the SAARC countries ranges from US $ 1165 in (Nepal) to US $ 3030 in (Sri Lanka). The annual growth rate of GDP ranges from 7.2 per cent (Maldives) and 3.7 per cent (Sri Lanka). Sri Lanka appeared to be the most inflationary country among SAARC countries with the rate of inflation touching 16.1 per cent during 1995-96, whereas it accounted only 3.1 per cent in case of Maldives. Further, the per capita exports and imports are highest, i.e. US $192 and US $ 1373 in case of Maldives and lowest, i.e. US $15.4 and 35.3 in case of Nepal. Thus, Nepal appears to be the least developed country of SAARC in terms of GDP and trade. The per capita foreign exchange excluding gold of the SAARC countries are highest, i.e. US $243.7 in case of Maldives and lowest, i.e. US $6.1 in case of Pakistan. However, the per capita foreign debt ranges from US $ 400 (Maldives) and US$ 55.2 (Bhutan). If we examine the exchange rate of currency per US $ of each country, the value of Maldives's Refiyaa was the highest, i.e. 13.14 and Nepali rupee was the lowest, i.e. 57.25.

Human Development report, authored by the distinguished Pakistani economist, Mahbub-ul-haq speaks volumes about the low profile quality of life in this region. Fifty years after independence, about 500 million people in the region are destitute; basic education is denied to 1200 million individuals and 260 million are without elementary health facilities. In terms of real per capita income, Pakistan ranks 119th and India 142nd in the world. In the face of such a grim situation in the social sector, says the report, the countries of South Asia are spending too much on arms and too little on the social sectors. India ranks first in total arm imports and Pakistan tenth, though India's per capita expenditure is far less than Pakistan's. While the global expenditure declined by 37 percent during the last decades, military spending in South Asia has gone up by 12 per cent during the same period. As far as the UNDP (United Nations Development Programme) Human development index is concerned SAARC countries occupied lowest positions. NCAER (National Council of Applied Economic Research) human development profile of India said that about 16 per cent of India's rural population earned rupees 3 per day and another 18 per cent about Rs 5 per day. Accessibility of safe drinking water is denied to nearly 50 per cent of the villagers. UNDP introduced the human development index[63] comprising life expectancy, educational attainments and income indicators to give a composite measure of human development. SAARC countries occupied low positions in this ranking. They were ranked as; Sri Lanka (89), Pakistan (134), India (135), Bangladesh (143), Nepal (151) and Bhutan (158).

Trade is one of the major priority areas of economic cooperation under the SAARC charter. In spite of various commonalities of SAARC countries, the intra-regional SAARC trade was 2.8 per cent of their global trade during 1985 which, however, picked up to 4 per cent till 1995 and then it progressed further. The operationalisation of SAARC preferential trading arrangement (SAPTA) on December 7, 1995, a decade after the launch of SAARC was of course a positive step in the right direction. In fact, it was the real beginning of SAARC, but at the same time it was only a first step towards a liberalisation and creation of SAARC trade block. The Consolidated National Schedules of Concessions containing the list of products furnished by the member countries for tariff concessions is not very impressive. In the first round of SAPTA negotiations, SAARC countries identified 226 items (484 tariff lines at six digit level) for exchange on tariff concessions ranging from 10 per cent to 100 per cent.[64] India agreed to extend tariff concessions to 50 per cent on106 items, while Pakistan agreed to offer tariff concessions from 10 per cent to 20 per cent on 35 items, Sri Lanka on 31 items, Maldives 75 per cent on 17 items, Nepal 10 per cent on 14 items, Bangladesh 10 per cent on 12 items and Bhutan 15 per cent on 11 items. However during the second round of SAPTA negotiations which concluded in Kathmandu on 29-30th November 1996, items for exchange on tariff concessions picked up the 1972 tariff lines from Brussels round.

India agreed to give tariff concessions on 911 items, while Pakistan offered tariff concessions on 368 items, Nepal on 227 tariff lines, Bangladesh on 241 tariff lines and Maldives on 8 tariff lines. The slow process of SAPTA is manifested with the fact that SAARC countries could finalise only 1972 tariff lines out of the 6000 tariff lines for tariff concessions.[65] However, there was a proposal of transition from SAPTA to SAFTA (SAARC free trade area) in the eighth SAARC summit in New Delhi with the total elimination of all tariff and non-tariff barriers by 2005. Keen interest shown by all the member countries of SAARC in the ninth SAARC summit held in Male during May 1997 advanced the deadline for the implementation of SAFTA from 1995 to 2001. India's proposal for SAEC (SAARC Economic Community) after attaining the goal of SAFTA had also been responded positively in this summit.

South Asia has recently undergone many developments that signify radical change. However, such improvements are not sufficient to meet the MDG's millennium development goals and other development goals. The region has the concentration of the poor people with more than 500 hundred million (a third of the regions poor people population) living on less than US $ 1.25 a day[66] with abject poverty, rising income inequalities and regional disparities remain issues of concern. Human deprivation is widespread in many parts of the region. Regional diversity born out of the multi-racial, multi-religious, multi-linguistic and multi-cultural cooperation adds further to the complexity of ensuring effective governance.

According to the latest HDI data published, the South Asian region falls at the bottom in the group of countries with medium human development since 1998 and continues to lag behind many other regions in the world. Further the gap between the region and the rest of the world does not seem to be reducing. The only region behind South Asia is sub-Saharan Africa. It is clear that human development has not kept up with the pace of economic growth in the region. Despite these low levels of human development most countries in South Asia have failed to enhance public allocations for education and health. Economic survey since has not led to any major improvement in public allocations to social services. Improvements in social indicators have been slow generally not only on the grounds of limited expenditure but because of low levels of efficiency in the delivery of social services.

Table IV: HDI (Human Development Index) for South Asia 2011

Country	*Value*	*Rank*
India	0.547	134
Pakistan	0.504	145
Bangladesh	0.500	146
Afghanistan	0.398	172
Nepal	0.458	157
Sri Lanka	0.691	97
Bhutan	0.522	141
Maldives	0.66	109

Source: UNDP 2011 (a).

To deal with some of these common problems, which the South Asian Region as a whole faces, the South Asian association for regional cooperation was launched in December 1985. SAARC is the manifestation of the determination of the people of South Asia to cooperate regionally and to work together towards finding solution of their common problems in a spirit of friendship; trust and understanding based on mutual respect, equality and shared benefits. The main motive behind SAARC is that the countries of South Asian region can achieve their objectives of all-round development more easily and more speedily, if they cooperate with each other.

Review of Literature

There is a vast literature available on SAARC as a regional organisation in particular and regionalism in general. This is an evolving organisation right from its birth in 1985, as it has been developing and taking new and new shape with the passage of time and holding of different summits. There is no dearth of material related to SAARC. The work *Contemporary South Asia* (1985) edited by Dharma Dasani and introduced by Ramakant provides general framework of the emerging issues and trends in South Asia. This work has also highlighted the role of external powers in South Asia and this has acted as a catalyst in the emergence of SAARC. Moreover this work also highlights the basic parameters of South Asian region. J.N. Dixit in his work on "*Indian Foreign Policy and its Neighbours*" (2005) highlights the India's role in SAARC and changing nature of India's foreign policy towards its immediate neighbours with the change in political leadership in India. He also mentions in his work that a basic shift took place in India's foreign policy after the Chinese aggression on India in 1962. India's policy of NAM (Non-alignment movement) received a severe jolt in 1971 when India override the principles of NAM and signed the treaty of peace, friendship and cooperation with Soviet Union. The last decade of the twentieth century and first two years of the present century have seen dramatic changes in global power equation, economic developments and the forward march of technology. India itself has gone through some political upheavals. Another Work "*Regionalism in South Asia: Negotiating Cooperation, Institutional Structures*", (2008) of Kishore C. Dash, provides brief information about the formation and working of regional cooperation. He argues that 'regional integration is a two level process'. The main focus of this book is on the factors that impact on the regional cooperation of South Asia. The author studies the process of cooperation building in South Asia, through the case study of SAARC; the author argues that SAARC was formed primarily to discuss the issues of peace and development in the South Asian region. The book also attempts to study the 'nature of domestic institutions and also mentioned the strength why states have failed in regional cooperative initiatives'. Another work "*Challenges and Strategy–Rethinking India's Foreign Policy*" (2009) by Rajiv Sikri which highlights difficulties of the regional cooperation under SAARC such as mutual suspicion, hostility and political hesitation. V.N. Khanna in his famous work on "*Foreign Policy of India*" (2010) expresses the doubts about the progress of regional organisation in the present era of globalisation and liberalisation. However according to Khanna, South Asia has untold potential for regional cooperation, which if exploited properly can lift the South Asia from the lower equilibrium trap of poverty to a greater spectrum of development. Another work "*South Asian Union: Problems, Possibilities and Prospects*" (2005) by Ranjit Kumar deftly highlights the origins and prospects of the new dream for reconnecting the people of the subcontinent and reintegrating its market. The work

"*India and the Regional Integration in South Asia*" (1964) by Sisir Gupta highlights India's attitude towards regional integration in South and South East Asia respectively. It also provides the insight of India towards the overall objectives and policies in foreign affairs, the role which India has played in various conferences of Asian states and in various efforts towards regional integration and the impact of domestic policies and the attitudes of Indian elite groups. The book also gives a glimpse of information regarding the impediments which came into action during the India's role in regional integration. The author feels that the process of regional integration should start in the Indo-Pakistan subcontinent, and he is convinced that India and Pakistan have between them the most fertile ground for attempted regional integration in Asia" but he realises that many impediments stand in the way of Indo-Pakistan cooperation. The work "*India's role in South Asian Regional Cooperation*" (1991) by Vyuptakesh Sharan provides the information about the origin of SAARC from its infancy. The work also tells us about bright and weak points of India in SAARC and suggests measures that aim at strengthening the weak linkages and thereby achieving the SAARC goals smoothly and within a prescribed time. "*The Dynamics of South Asia Regional Cooperation and SAARC*" (1999) an edited work by Eric Gonsalves and Nancy Jetly advocates the need for enhancing dialogue between the countries of South Asia in order to find a common ground. Tackling issues of considerable importance both at the regional and global level, the work is an extended in mapping out interstate relations in the areas of political relations, security concerns, technological and commercial issues, intellectual and cultural commonalities and the impact of foreign aid. The contributors stress the importance of economic and cultural linkages and the need for South Asia to reinvent its regional agenda on the basis of cooperation and mutual understanding. "*South Asia: The Spectre of Terrorism*" (2009) by P R Kumaraswamy and Ian Copland looks at the ongoing debates that are taking place within South Asia regarding terrorism, and how these shape the approaches towards fighting terrorism. This work also highlights various terrorism-related problems and developments in the subcontinent and offers a new and unconventional understanding of the problem. "*SAARC; Relevance in new World Order*" (2003) by Farhat Ehsaas is useful work related to SAARC. It provides us information about the different aspects of the regional organisation in South Asia covering the organisations background, growth, problems, issues and prospects with objectivity and rationality in mind. *"India's Foreign Policy Continuity and Change*" (1979) edited by Bimal Prasad is a classic work on India's foreign policy which not only deals with the theme of continuity and change in India's foreign policy but also trace the evolution of this policy since 1947 and elucidate and analyse its various aspects and its operation in relation to the different countries and regions of the world. "*SAARC and Globalisation: Issues, Prospects and Policy Prescriptions*" (2008) by Hussain Mohi-ud-Din Qadri sheds light on the various aspects of globalisation in relation to SAARC. This book presents the challenges posed to the South Asian region and made recommendations to transform these challenges into opportunities to offset the negative implications of globalisation and use it in the larger interest of its people. This book also discusses the politico-economic issues facing Pakistan in particular and the region in general. The implication here is that political conditions impact upon the economic health of a country very deeply and as long as political house is not set in order, economic well-being cannot be achieved. This book presents a model for economic integration of South Asia in light of experiences of regional groupings like European Union, AFA and NAFTA etc. *"South Asia: In Search of a Regional Identity"* (1991) by R P Anand describes South Asian a 'region without regionalism' despite having the commonalities and similarities, these countries have not been able to come together. At the end this work also shows us how South Asian countries are trying to come together through SAARC and how this small step can help them to start on a long road towards cooperation despite all the asymmetrical and disparate relations prevailing among them. "*SAARC; Through the New Millennium*" (2003) edited by Yudhistar Kahol covers all the aspects and future prospects of the organisation. At least about eleven summits have been accounted in detail in this work. This work also deals about the India's role in South Asia and also its big brother attitude towards its regional small neighbours and also prescribes towards a united South Asia. "*South Asia Envisioning a Regional Future*" (2010) the work edited by Smruti S Pattanaik is related with the issues that challenge the region and individual states in the region and how external powers influence and in what way the region gets affected because of outside powers and moreover the role of regional institutional mechanisms in fostering cooperation and greater economic integration in a globalised world, where connectivity is a key. It is recognised that the region suffers from several constraints that has made common challenges difficult to address. Nevertheless there is an optimism that in course of history the region will move forward steadily and smoothly provided they give secondary importance to issues of conflict for a while and adhere to the thought of socio-economic development in a world where everything is governed keeping economic interest in mind and shape a regional identity that would form the bedrock of any cooperative endeavour. "*The Politics of Extremism in South Asia*" (2008) written by Deepa Ollapally examines extremist groups in Kashmir, Afghanistan, Northeast India, Pakistan, Bangladesh and Sri Lanka to offer a fresh perspective on the cause of extremism. How they arise in societies which are predisposed to extremism. How we can determine the gainers and losers in this all sort of troubled region. At last it also covers the theme that politics, inter-state and international relations often play a more important role in the rise of extremism in South Asia than religious identity, poverty and state deprivation.

SAARC is the manifestation of the determination of the people of South Asia to cooperate regionally and to work together towards finding solution of their common problems in a spirit of friendship; trust and understanding based on mutual respect, equality and shared benefits. The main motive behind SAARC is that, the countries of South Asian region can achieve their objectives of all-round development more easily and more speedily, if they cooperate with each other.

Notes

1. Morgenthau, H.J., (1948), *"Politics among Nations: The Struggle for Power and Peace"*, Knopf, New York, pp.15-16.
2. Padelford, Norman J (1954), "Regional Organizations and the United Nations", *International Organization*, pp.203-16
3. Mitrany, David (1996), *"A Working Peace System"*, Quadrangle Books, Chicago, pp. 35-36.

4. Nye, J.S. (1969), "*Inter Regionalism: Readings*" Little Brown, Boston, p. 8.
5. Mehotra, Nitasha, (2007): "*South Asia –Political and Economic Region*", The Association for Geographical Studies, Delhi University, New Delhi, pp. 5-6
6. *SAARC 2015 Expanding Horizons and Forging Cooperation in a Resurgent Asia*, the New Delhi Statement on SAARC 2015 and Asian Resurgence Friedrich-Ebert-Stiftung India Office, New Delhi.
7. *Ibid.*
8. *Ibid.*
9. Anand, R.P. (1991), "*South Asia: In search of a Regional Identity*", Banyan Publications, New Delhi, p. 1.
10. Shukla, Vijay (1996), "New Frontiers of SAARC", *India Quarterly, A Journal of International Affairs*, New Delhi, Vol.52, no.1-2, pp. 87-94.
11. Mishra, K.P. (1995), "South Asian Regional Security: Political and Socio-Economic dimension," *Punjab journal of politics,* Vol. 9, no.1, Punjab, p. 102.
12. Chanana, Charanjit (1976), "South Asia–An Economic Fraternity" *South Asian Survey*, Vol.1, no.2, New Delhi, p. 5.
13. Mohanan, B. (1992), "*The Politics of Regionalism in South Asia*", Atlantic Publishers, New Delhi, p. 27.
14. Chandra Prakash and Arora Prem, (1983), "*International Relations: Foreign Policies of Major Powers and Regional Systems*", Vikas Publishers, New Delhi, p. 237.
15. Geography of South Asia, at http//;www.en.wikipedia.org/wiki/South Asia
16. *Ibid.*
17. Hagerty, Devin T., (2005), "*South Asia in World Politics*," Oxford University Press, New Delhi, p. 6.
18. *Ibid.*
19. Devabhaktuni, Sony (1997), "Regional Cooperation in South Asia: Prospects and Problems," *Occasional Paper*, no. 32, the Henry L. Stimson Center, Washington DC, pp. 1-3.
20. Www. *South Asian history net online* .co. in
21. Jha, Nalini Kant (2003), *"South Asia in 21st Century"*, South Asian Publishers, New Delhi, p. 70.
22. *Ibid.*
23. Mehotra, Nitasha (2007): *"South Asia –Political and Economic Region",* The Association for Geographical Studies, Delhi University, New Delhi, pp. 15-16.

24. Mehotra, Nitasha (2007): *"South Asia –Political and Economic Region"*, The Association for Geographical Studies, Delhi University, New Delhi, pp. 21-23.
25. Lodhi, Maheela (2001), *"View Point: Security Challenges in South Asia, the Non-proliferation" Review*, summer, p. 11.
26. Upreti, B.C. (2000), *"SAARC; Dynamics of Regional Cooperation in South Asia"*, Kalinga publications, Vol.2, New Delhi, pp. 151-152.
27. Qureshi, M.L,(1984), "*South Asian Economies during 1970s; An overall View"*, South Asian Studies, Lahore, Pakistan, Vol.1, p. 11.
28. Geography of South Asia, at http;/www.en.wikipedia-org/Wikipedia-Org/wiki/South.
29. Naqash, Nasir Ahmad, (1994), *SAARC: Challenges and Opportunities*, Ashish Publishing House, New Delhi, p. 12.
30. Bhanot, Monica (1999), "Challenges to Regional Cooperation in South Asia: A New Perspective," *Online Journal of Peace and Conflict*, at http://www.trinstitite.org/ojpcr,issue.
31. World Bank Report-2004 at http:/www.worldbank.org/report/WDR2004
32. United Nations International Children's Emergency Fund, an agency of United Nations Organisation to cater for the well being of the children's in the world.
33. Vandana, Mohla (1998), *"SAARC and Superpowers"*, Deep and Deep Publishers, New Delhi, pp. 41-42.
34. Kumaraswamy, P. R. and Copland, Ian (2009), "*South Asia the Spectre of terrorism*," Rutledge, New Delhi, pp. 23-24.
35. Jha, Nalini Kant (2003), *"South Asia in 21st Century*," South Asian Publishers, New Delhi, no. 22, p. 67.
36. Mehotra, Nitasha(2007), *"South Asia –Political and Economic Region",* The Association for Geographical Studies, Delhi University, New Delhi, pp. 5-6.
37. Lodi, Mahela (2001), "*View Point: Security Challenges in South Asia, the Non-proliferation*" *Review*, summer, no.15, p. 11.
38. Sridhar, K. Khatri and Gert W. Kueck,(2003), "*Terrorism in South Asia: Impacts on Development and Democratic Process*" RCSS Colombo, Konrad Adenauer Foundation & Shipra Publications, New Delhi, p. 67.
39. Jha, Nalini Kant (2003), "*South Asia in 21st Century*," South Asian Publishers, New Delhi, p. 67.

40. Treaty of Peace and Friendship between India and Nepal is a major point of debate between these two as it completely ignores Nepal's right to decide anything on its own sphere. Some academicians of international law believe that the treaty itself was illegal because it was signed by the Care Taker Prime Minister of Nepal in his final retreat from the state affairs just to appease Indian rulers.

41. Ganguly, Sumit (2003), "*India; As an Emerging Power*," Frank Cass, New Delhi, pp. 32-33.
42. Sahadevan, P. (2004), "India and Sri Lanka: A Changing Relationship," *Dialogue*, Vol. 5, n.3, New Delhi, pp. 143-145.
43. Kodikara, Shelton U. (1989), *"Indo-Sri Lankan Agreement of July 1987*," Colombo, University of Colombo, pp. 54-70.
44. Jha, Nalini Kant, (2003), *"South Asia in 21st Century",* South Asian Publishers, New Delhi, no. 22, p. 67.
45. Hagerty, Devin T. (2005), *South Asia in World Politics*, Oxford University Press, New Delhi, p. 7.
46. Chandra, D Bhatta, "Regional Integration and Peace in South Asia: An Analysis," at http; www. *Peacestudiesjournal* Org.UK/docs/regional integration. pdf.o2K
47. Upreti, B.C. (2009), "*SAARC; Dynamics of Regional Cooperation in South Asia*," Kalinga Publications, New Delhi, p. 59
48. South Asian Regional Cooperation at http//www.Southasianmedia.net
49. Mangi, Abdul Qayum, (2005), "Prospects of Social Charter among SAARC Countries," *Pakistan Horizon*, Karachi, Vol. 58, no. I. p. 62.
50. *Making services for poor people*, The World Development Report 2004, www.worldbank.org/reports./WDR2004
51. Mahbub-Ul-Haq Human Development Centre, "*Human Development in South Asia 1999; The Crisis of Governance",* Karachi; Oxford University Press, 2000, p. 2.
52. Hussain Akaml (2003), *Pakistan; National Human Development Report 2003*; at http;//www.undp.org/hdr2003
53. *World Development Report and Economic Survey of Pakistan*, 2002-2003.
54. Mahbub Ul Haq, *Human Development Center, Human Development in South Asia 2002; Agriculture and Rural Development* Report, Karachi; Oxford University Press, 2003, p. 232.
55. *Ibid.*
56. Maddawatta Priyadarshana (1999), "*Human Development Report shows worsening poverty in South Asia"*, at http;//www.wsws.org/articles/sasa-n29.html
57. *Millennium Development Goals Report 2011: Regional Press Release,* issued by UN Department of Public Information, New York, July 2011.
58. Human Development Report 2013, The Rise of the South: Human Progress in a Diverse World.
59. *Ibid.*
60. *Ibid.*
61. *Ibid.*

62. Mangi Abdul Qayum (2005), *"Prospects of Social Charter among SAARC Countries*", Pakistan Horizon, Karachi, Vol. 58, p. 69.
63. http://www.adb.org/sites/default/files/pub/2012/ado2012.pdf
64. Mukherji, I.N. (1996), "*South Asian Preferential Trading Arrangement: Assessing Trade Flows in the First Round of Trade Negotiations*", Friedrich, Naumann Stiftung, New Delhi.
65. *Ibid*.
66. World Bank 2012 h

Chapter - 2

Regional Organisations

The geo-political world continues to spin and turn every two or three years. The international situation gets transformed from decade to decade, and sometimes even during shorter periods. It would need a strong sense of perception to fully appreciate the coming events, but a careful, balanced and rational approach can enhance our understanding and reduce the threat from hidden dangers.[1] The idea of a political community cutting across state boundaries of global citizenship of economic integration among states is not new in international politics. This has been in existence right from the dawn of the history in one way or the other. Ever since the modern state system came into being, rather than functioning as self-contained units, the states have cooperated with each other to deal with various issues of common interest and concern. While earlier such cooperation took the shape of military alliances to counter potential adversaries, however with advancement in global communication and revolution in information technology, more and more state's realised the need of greater economic cooperation and mutual interdependence as a means for global peace and harmony.

The world today is at a turning point and the changes that we are undergoing are global in scope, revolutionary, fundamental and structural in content. As we have entered the twenty-first century a sense of optimism prevails for attaining peace and prosperity because of the role played by regional as well as global organisations. Due to the revolution in communication and transportation, the earth has shrunk and distances have virtually minimised. In such a state of affairs the meaning and contours of international relations and politics are changing. Presently the relevance of traditional barriers and traditional security is losing its focus; on the other hand its human security which is coming on the forefront is getting more and more attention. Hence a tendency of concentration and unity beyond borders is gaining ground.[2] Various nations are joining hands for creating a common forum or group in order to protect their secondary interests be it commercial, cultural and political. Regional cooperation is fast emerging as key link in man's thirst for peace, development and excellence. Number of countries with different national loyalties and being heterogeneous in certain aspects and with different levels of growth and development are looking for ways of building up regional cooperation.[3]

The process of forming these supra national and extra territorial organisations got its practical shape in the form of UNO (United Nations Organisation) in 1945 after the end of World War II. The UNO represents the common aspirations of mankind. It was first and most important organisation emerged with the following main objectives:

(i) To save succeeding generations from the scourge of war, which twice in our lifetime has brought untold sorrow to mankind;

(ii) To reaffirm faith in the fundamental human rights in the dignity and worth of the human person, in the equal rights of men and women and of nations, large and small;

(iii) To establish conditions under which justice and respect for the obligations arising from treaties and other sources of international law can be maintained;

(iv) To promote social progress and better standard of life among newly independent countries.[4]

South Asia is a macro geographical region wherein various countries in close geographical proximity share certain commonalities or interests. The region is diverse in all considerations of security and insecurity. Perhaps no other region in the world is as contentious in its relations with each other as the South Asian region. The departure of colonial rule from this region gave birth to twins' independence and disputes. To replace and to somehow manage the intensity of these disputes and to achieve cooperation in this part of the world, a sort of regional set up was created in South Asia, namely the South Asian Association of Regional Cooperation.

Emergence of SAARC

South Asian association of regional cooperation is an association of South Asian countries to enhance their social progress, cultural development and political stability of the region. Formerly, it has seven members but from 2007 with the addition of Afghanistan the membership has gone up to eight. The original members of the organisation were Bangladesh, Bhutan, India, Maldives, Nepal, Pakistan and Sri Lanka. It was formed in December, 1985 by the initiative of late Bangladeshi president, Zia Ur Rehman.

SAARC is relatively recent and one of the later step in the chronology of regional groupings. SAARC may be seen as a new member of the family of regional organisations in the world. On the closer look, it appears to be distinct and different from many other such regional groupings like the European Economic Community (EEC), The Economic Community of West Asian States (ECOWAS), Association of South East Asian Nations (ASEAN), etc. due to some distinctive features of the South Asian region.[5]

The creation of the South Asian association of regional cooperation in 1985 represented the recognition of the geopolitical entity of South Asia. The methodologies used for identifying the regional area as consisting of geographically proximate and interacting states sharing some degree of common ethnic, linguistic, cultural, social and historical bonds become the basis of the formation of the association. The countries included in this regional organisation are Afghanistan, Bangladesh, Bhutan, India, Maldives, Nepal, Pakistan and Sri Lanka.

Before the creation of SAARC, idea of regional cooperation in South Asia was discussed in at least three Conferences. The Asian Relations Conferences in New Delhi in April 1947, the Bangui Conferences in the Philippines in May 1950 and the Colombo Conference in April 1954.[6]

The concept of South Asian regional integration, when viewed in a broader concept of regional development in Asia represents a second wave of regionalism. The first wave of this process had commenced by the late 1940's with the convening of first Asian relations conference.[7]

President Zia Ur Rehman after the visit of Nepal, India, Pakistan and Sri Lanka during the period of 1977-1978 proposed the possibilities of regional economic cooperation among the South Asian countries. He proposed for the collective self-reliance in a common quest for peace and development of all the countries of the region. In May 1980 he issued a formal letter for all the SAARC countries (India, Pakistan, Sri Lanka, Nepal, Bhutan and Maldives). This call received a positive response from all these countries. Though India and Pakistan were initially hesitant to accept the proposal, India feared that Zia Ur Rehman's idea might provide an opportunity for the small neighbouring countries of the region to regionalize all bilateral issues and join with each other to gang up against India, Pakistan seemed to be apprehensive of the Bangladesh initiative because it thought that it will result in the economic and political domination of India in the region. However, after a series of quite diplomatic consultations between the foreign ministers of the region at the United Nations headquarters in New York from August to September 1980, it was agreed that Bangladesh would prepare the draft of a working paper for discussion among the foreign secretaries of the region (South Asia). The new Bangladesh draft paper, aware of India and Pakistan concerns dropped all references to security matters and suggested only non-political and non-controversial areas for cooperation.[8] Several factors seemed to have prompted Zia Ur Rehman to take this initiative for establishing a regional Cooperation in South Asia. These were:

(i) Change in the political leadership in the South Asian countries and demonstrations of accommodative diplomacy by the new leaders.

(ii) Zia Ur Rehman's need for Indian support to legitimise his coup d'état regime.

(iii) An acute balance of payment crisis of almost all the South Asian countries, which was further aggravated by the second oil crisis in 1979.

(iv) Failure of the North-South dialogue and increasing protectionism by the developed countries.

(v) Publication of an extremely useful background report by the Committee on Studies for Cooperation in Development in South Asia (CSCD) identifying many feasible areas of cooperation.

(vi) Assurance of economic assistance for multi-lateral cooperative projects on sharing water resources of Ganga and Brahmaputra by United States President Jimmy Carter and British Prime Minister James Callaghan during their visit to India, Pakistan and Bangladesh in January 1978.

(vii) The Soviet Union's military intervention in Afghanistan in December 1979 resulting in rapid deterioration of the South Asian security situation.[9]

For the proposed cooperation among the South Asian countries, consultations were carried out at the official level. The consultations brought out clearly that regional cooperation in the South Asian region should on the one hand, reflect the spirit of mutual trust, understanding and sympathetic appreciation of the political inspiration existing among the countries of the region and on the other hand, such cooperation should be based on the principle of sovereign equality, territorial integrity, non-interference in internal affairs of other nations and mutual benefits.[10] Between 1980 and 1983, four meetings were held at the foreign secretary level, to establish the principle of organisation and identify areas for Cooperation.[11] After three years of preparatory discussions at the official level, the first South Asian foreign ministers conferences were held in New Delhi from August 1-3,1983 where the Integrated Programme of Action on mutually agreed areas of cooperation i.e., agriculture, rural development, telecommunications, meteorology, health and population control, transport, sports, art and culture, postal services and science and technology was launched.

The Charter of South Asian association for regional cooperation (SAARC) consists of preamble and ten articles.

The preamble defines the principles for which the SAARC is formed. These include promoting peace, stability and adherence to the principles of United Nations and principles of Non-aligned Movement (NAM). It reaffirms the commitment for sovereign equality, territorial independence, non-use of force and non-interference in the internal affairs of other states and peaceful settlement of all disputes.[12]

Article I explains the main objectives of SAARC. The main objectives are to promote the welfare of the people of the region and to improve their quality of life to accelerate economic growth, to promote active collaboration and mutual assistance in the economic, social and cultural, technical and scientific fields to promote mutual trust and appreciation of one another's problems and to cooperate with international and regional organisations.[13]

The third section of the charter (Article II) explains the principles and modulations of its functioning. SAARC abides by the principles of sovereign equality, territorial integrity and non-interference in the internal affairs of other states. Besides this, it (SAARC) is not to substitute for bilateral and multi-lateral obligations.[14]

The next section comprising of Articles III to VIII deals with organisational issues. The SAARC charter made a provision for a four tier structure with a permanent secretariat. The apex of the summit i.e., the heads of states or governments meets annually.[15] The charter also provided for a council of ministers consisting of foreign ministers, who were required to meet as often as possible, to formulate policies of the association, to revive the progress of cooperation and to identify new areas of cooperation.[16] The charter provides for a standing committee of foreign secretaries of participating countries for an overall monitoring and coordination of programmes of cooperation; for approving projects and programmes and modalities of financing determination of inter-sectoral priorities and identification of new areas. The standing committee is to meet as often as necessary. It has to submit reports to the council of ministers.[17]

To assist the standing committee, a provision was also made for a technical committee, comprising representatives of member states. These committees have to determine the potential and scope of regional cooperation in agreed areas, formulate programmes, prepare projects and determine financial implications of inter-sectoral programmes.[18]

The charter also provides for setting up of an action committee for assisting standing committee and for implementation of projects involving more than two but not all member states.[19]

Under Article VIII, SAARC charter also provides for a secretariat which is headed by a secretary general at the ambassador's level. The SAARC secretariat was formally inaugurated in Kathmandu (Nepal) in January 1987. The secretariat comprises the secretary general, seven directors and the general service staff. The secretariat serves as the channel of communication between SAARC and other regional and international organisations and coordinates day-to-day activities. In the SAARC charter, it has been left to the council of ministers to finalise its organisation, functions and funding modalities.[20]

Article IX deals with financial arrangements the contribution of each country is voluntary. The technical committees shall make recommendations for the apportionment of costs of implementing the programmed proposed by it. The external financing may be mobilised by the standing committee.

Article X lays down the decision-making process which has to be made on the basis of unanimity. Further it states that bilateral and contentious issues are to be excluded by SAARC.

One of the most important developments in world politics in the post-world war second period has been the proliferation of regional organisations of varied nature and scope, and the experience has shown that this process has contributed a lot to the world in terms of economic, political and social progress.

However, the success of SAARC depends upon the mutual trust among all the member states. It is required that fear psychosis, suspicion and jealousy among the member countries should be removed. Thus, SAARC has been an important step in the direction of Regional Cooperation in South Asia. Synergy in conflict management and optimising Cooperation in Asia is a skill to be mastered and an ideal never to be lost from sight of those committed to peace and Cooperation in Asia.

The formation of SAARC was responded differently from different quarters of the region. Jigme Singye Wangchuck, King of Bhutan described it as a manifestation of collective wisdom and political will to bring about meaningful regional cooperation in spite of the differences on foreign policy and security perspectives. On the other hand the then president Zia-Ul-Haq of Pakistan expressed apprehensions about the dominant position of India which could deter the fulfillment of the objectives and ideals of SAARC. Similar misgivings were entertained by other smaller countries. These misgivings arise due to the size and population of India. Prem Aurora writes "it is desirable that India should try to allay these feelings by demonstrating both by words and deeds that she will always be ready to enter into constructive and mutually beneficial cooperation with other countries as may seek it".[21] South Asia being one of the most geographically integrated regions in the world is least integrated for regionalism as compared with Europe, Africa, South East Asia and North and South America. The geographical reality of the region is that India has common land and maritime borders with all the countries of the South Asian region. India constitutes the central hub of the region along with asymmetry in size, resources, and capabilities. The Indo-Centrality approach to South Asia has given a feeling of insecurity among the states of the region. India believes in friendship and cooperation among neighbours and in this regard smaller nations of South Asia have an opportunity for their development by cooperating with India.

India's Role in Regional Cooperation

During the India's struggle for freedom, close collaboration with Asian countries became one of the basic objectives of the national movement. The anti-pathy to European imperialism often leads to an uncritical glorification of the role of other Asian countries in the world. For example, one of the anti-British movements in India–the Khilafat-was built around the Indian Muslims dissatisfaction with the disintegration of the Ottoman Empire.[22] In 1920, Gandhi wrote about the growing solidarity of the Asian countries. Again in 1922, C.R. Das, while presiding over the Indian National Congress, urged Indian participation in an Asian federation as inevitable. The slogan for

Eastern federation was given by great Muslim leader, Muhammad Ali while presiding over the Congress in 1923.[23] The need for an Asian federation was again emphasised in 1926 Congress session. Long before Nehru became Prime Minister in his first speech on foreign policy in December 1927 at the annual convention of the Congress party, he stated that 'the people of India have no quarrel with their neighbours and desires to live at peace with them'.[24] To give practical shape to it a resolution was carried out in 1928. The statements regarding Asian Unity continued during those days. The two countries besides India which were involved in the movement of Asian unity were Japan and Soviet Union respectively. The general expressions of sympathy and moreover a degree of exchange of ideas and opinions among the nationalists of Asia and regular sessions of Indian National Congress received messages and expectations of support from other Asian countries like the Wafd party of Egypt[25], the Kuomintang of China and the Burmese national leaders. The movement towards regionalism did not create any institutional arrangements in Asia. This remained as an effort in identifying the common concerns of post-colonial states focusing on the problems of development. Even before India became formally free, the leaders of the national movement took steps to convene the Asian relations conference in Delhi in 1947. The tone for the conference was set by Nehru in his inaugural speech or address to the conference. The four major agendas covering the theme of the conference were the proclamation of Asia's arrival on the world scene, the stress on the need for Asian unity, the need to avoid the expression of anti-western sentiments and the need for greater regional cooperation.

India emerged as the leader of the non-aligned movement in the post-colonial twentieth century. The Indian policy of non-alignment in respect of South Asia was intended to limit the penetration of cold war politics into the region. India's political position in the world in general and Asia in particular suffered serious setback in 1960's on account of deterioration in relations with China resulting in the humiliating war of 1962. Further the drought and agricultural failure during third five year plan (1961-66), brought India on the brink of an economic collapse. India had to import food to prevent starvation and the World Bank in 1966 enforced devaluation of Indian currency.[26]

There was a widespread impression in the west that India would not survive long as a united country, and would not be able to feed itself and develop as a viable state.[27] But later events particularly India's decisive victory against Pakistan in 1971 war resulting in creation of Bangladesh, achievement of self-sufficiency in food production and nuclear test explosion at Pokhron (1974) restored India's credibility and image in international power politics.

In the context of prevailing political and security environment in South Asia and the mindset of its neighbours, India apprehended that the initiative for South Asian regional cooperation might be an attempt to build a disguised anti-Soviet and pro-US strategic front. India wanted withdrawal of Soviet troops from Afghanistan, but at the same time was against any US moves which could have brought fierce superpower rivalry in the region. Moreover there was apprehensions in India, given the history of political disputes in the region, that the proposed regional forum might be used by her neighbours to gang up against her and try to settle disputes to her disadvantage.[28] The proposal to counter such apprehensions put forth that the experience of regional cooperation in other parts of the world indicated the possibility of such cooperation despite bilateral problems among the countries of the region. Rather, it was maintained that as regional cooperation would grow, it would generate a climate of mutual understanding reducing the scope for such disputes.[29] The proposal by Bangladesh listed several possible areas of cooperation in the fields of agriculture, science and technology, transport market promotion, education and culture. A draft deceleration proposed to be adopted by the countries to launch the regional forum appended with this proposal mentioned promotion of peace and stability in the region through adherence to principles of United Nations charter and non-alignment as the objectives of regional cooperation in South Asia. It also expressed determination to uphold respect for the principles of sovereignty, national independence, territorial integrity, non-interference in one another's internal affairs, non-use of force and peaceful settlement of disputes.[30]

India's role in promoting regionalism in South Asia can be viewed in the light of the hindrances, the roots of conflict and the recent developments. It is a well-known fact that the Indian leaders always visualised a major role for India not just in the subcontinent but in Asia and in the third world as a whole. India has always been committed to regional cooperation in the economic, political, social, technological and cultural spheres. The concept of regionalism is rather a new phenomenon in international politics. It was not thought by the founding fathers of the United Nations. They favoured a universal approach towards restructuring the war-torn international community. This mindset was shared by Jawaharlal Nehru who elaborated this vision in one of his speeches in September 1946: "The world in spite of its rivalries and hatreds and inner conflicts, moves inevitably towards closer cooperation and the building up of a world commonwealth. It is for this one world that free India will work, a world in which there is the free cooperation of free people, and no class or group exploits another".[31] India in particular was perceived as being qualified to promote this idea. Its rich civilisational heritage enabled the country to contribute basic guidelines for peaceful cooperation, the famous formula of Panchsheel. The principles as such were not new, but the idea to make them the basis of practical state policy and conduct in international relations was unique. Pundit Jawaharlal Nehru in his foreign policy statements during the first decade of independence repeatedly stressed that nurturing peace is not merely an abstention from war but that it involved encouragement of continuously expanding cooperation between nations, particularly of the Asian region. This commitment of India at the macro level has psychological and political constraint. Regardless of India's professions and advocacies of cooperation, all of India's neighbours had apprehensive perceptions about India. Therefore, while advocating regional cooperation India did not make any proposal for institutional arrangements for this purpose because it anticipated suspicion, even resistance from its neighbours, if India were to take the initiative in the matter. This was dictated by India's geographical placement, historical experiment and power potential. The disparity in size, demography, resources and levels of development between India on the one hand and all its neighbours on the other led to this approach. The additional factor of a number of political issues on which there were and are controversies between India and its neighbours underpinned India's reticence in this matter. Hence, it was with caution that India viewed the proposal for South Asian regional cooperation put forth by the late Bangladeshi president, Zia Ur Rehman in January 1980. There was the perception that in view of the perennial tensions between India and Pakistan and the distance which characterised India's relations with Bangladesh and Sri Lanka, his proposal would be a purely cosmetic experience. There was also the apprehension that the forum, if created would be a regional platform for India bashing-for putting collective pressure on India on matters of individual concerns to each of the other participant countries. Nonparticipation would have laid India open to the accusation of scuttling an innovative proposal for regional cooperation, despite being the most socio-economically endowed country in the region. SAARC has had a chequerred history ever since due to political controversies, impinging negatively on areas where there could have been meaningful cooperation. SAARC countries have to evolve a practical framework and realistic terms of reference for cooperation in substantive matters of mutual benefit, based on mutual complementarity. Future prospects depend on whether South Asian countries can make this beginning and then move on to concrete interaction. Nehru once said, "India is very curiously placed in Asia, and her history has been influenced in a great deal by the geographical factor plus other factors. Whichever problem in Asia you may take up somehow or other India comes in to the picture. She cannot be ignored also because of her actual or potential power and resources".[32] In the very first meeting of foreign secretaries, Indian foreign secretary R.D. Sathe while reacting cautiously to the Bangladeshi proposal said, "We fully subscribe to the view expressed therein that in the foreseeable future, regional cooperation in South Asia has to be confined to economic, technical, scientific, social and cultural fields. It is inevitable that there will be some differences of emphasis if not perception in regard to a preliminary document of this nature. We feel that till detailed examination has taken place it would be premature to consider the institutionalisation of regional cooperation through the establishment of a secretariat, etc."[33] Further in a very forth right and pragmatic manner Indian foreign secretary, R.D. Sathe put forth two important preconditions for regional cooperation in South Asia when he said:

At this stage it would also be useful to stress that we reach unequivocal agreement on what I would call the ground rules, which should govern regional cooperation exercise and which in fact appear in the Bangladesh paper itself. Here I would submit that the principle of avoiding discussion in regional framework of all bilateral and contentious issues and of unanimity as the principle on the basis of which decisions in regard to regional cooperation are taken should be followed scrupulously. This meeting in Colombo agreed for the need of regional cooperation as a complement of already existing bilateral and multi-lateral cooperation among the countries of South Asia. It decided to proceed gradually on the basis of careful and adequate preparation for early realisation of such cooperation. Indian foreign secretary, R.D. Sathe, gave a firm and clear indication of India's policy of gradual movement towards regionalism in South Asia while concluding his speech in the first meeting he said' "we have an obligation to lay a solid and secure foundation on which regional cooperation can be built." If there are delays one should not become pessimistic, Rome was not built in a day. Neither was other regional groupings established without several meetings and through discussions. In fact, I would submit that while we should no doubt profit from the experience of other regions in the world. A pattern of regional cooperation in South Asia should evolve itself, we do not have to jump steps ahead and create an organisational superstructure without first agreeing upon arrangements, modalities and programmes of regional cooperation". The second meeting of foreign secretaries was held at Kathmandu, Nepal during November 2-4, 1981. In this meeting Indian foreign secretary R.D. Sathe went to say, when we have worked out a substantial programme of cooperation, we should move in the direction of recommending to our foreign ministers to convene a meeting at their level in order to launch such a programme and to provide guidance for further progress. The Indian foreign secretary, M. Rasgotra, in accordance with his country's cautious and step by step approach and about the meetings to be convened at the level of foreign ministers cautioned that, "At our level we have some important progress. A lot more remains to be done, we have yet to complete our task of presenting to the ministers a concrete and comprehensive action oriented programme including specific measures for its coordination and implementation. For this a few more meetings at our level would seem necessary, though this need not mean an unduly, extended time frame for the meeting at the level of foreign ministers."[34] However, Indian suggestion was not acceptable to Pakistan, Bangladesh and Nepal. In addition to the argument against venturing into too many fields, too soon, an underlying streak of apprehension of India's domination in these fields, particularly in the field of trade and industry, might also possibly be the factor behind this stance.

Political Push for South Asian Regionalism (1983-85)

The process for regional cooperation in South Asia moved a significant step further when the foreign secretaries decided to raise the level of interaction to the political plane.[35] The two important conditions reflecting Indian position were incorporated as General provisions under the institutional arrangements, vis, decisions at all levels would be taken on the basis of unanimity, and bilateral and contentious issues would be excluded from the deliberations. Further the Indian position towards regional cooperation was appropriately articulated by the then Prime Minister of India Indira Gandhi in her inaugural address to the meeting of the foreign ministers. Indian Prime Minister Mrs. Indira Gandhi while underlining the commonalities of geography, experiences, aspirations, challenges and civilisation also talked of each countries individual personality, distinctive perception and a different political system. She further affirmed; 'Our policy is not to interfere in the affairs of others. But ours is a troubled region, most of our countries are multi-racial and multi religious. It would be idle to pretend that we are not affected by what happens elsewhere. Even as we meet, there are disturbing and tragic developments in our neighbourhhood'.[36] On the crucial issue of summit meeting of SAARC countries, Indian foreign minister Bali Ram Bhagat observed: "Obviously such a meeting will require thorough preparation so that we are in a position to put something concrete before our leaders. Before we initiate the preparatory process, we would need to have a clear perception of what we should aim to achieve at the summit."[37] India obviously was not in a hurry to hold the summit meeting. It was agreed to recommend the respective head of state or government that the first summit of South Asian countries be held in Dhaka in the last quarter of 1985 to be preceded by a meeting of the foreign ministers in Bhutan in May 1985 to serve as the preparatory meeting of the summit. It was held against the backdrop of heightened tension between India and Sri Lanka over Tamil problem. On the most important issue of summit meeting, Indian minister of state for external affairs, Indira Gandhi who was also the prime minister at the point of time, for external affairs clarified his government's position as, the scope of SARC activities grows, we must ensure that we have an adequate framework to provide the necessary institutional support. This will be an important issue before the first SAARC summit to be held in this year. It is a matter of satisfaction that a consensus has been reached at the standing committee that a South Asian Association for Regional Cooperation will be created. My delegation is in favour of a council of ministers and the establishment of a secretariat at the appropriate time. While extending full support to the evolving process of South Asian regionalism Indian minister sounded a note of caution and said, "I would like to conclude by affirming once again our full support for the further evolution of SAARC- both conceptually and institutionally. We extend our hand in solidarity, knowing fully that what we are seeking to achieve cannot be done with ease. The present international scene continues to be dictated by noble platitudes and harsh realities. History has shown that even when benefits 'of working together are positive and self-evident, vested and narrow interests tend to entangle the gains that could accrue from such cooperation we must increase our self-reliance and reduce our susceptibilities' to pressures both within and outside our control. Divided we are vulnerable, united we will move forward to a bright future in pursuit of freedom and peace so essential for it." An important characteristic of this region is it is Indo-centric nature. India is central to the whole region and this is not only so in terms of India's geographical location and contagious boundaries with neighbours but also with respect to socio-cultural identities and experiences of historical and political evolution. Commonalities in South Asia are mostly bilateral between India and each of the neighbouring countries separately and individually. India in the third meeting was keen to incorporate tourism and trade as the areas of cooperation in the agenda. Indian foreign secretary, M. Rasgotra mentioned trade as a field of great importance for regional cooperation. He said in fact in many other regions of the world, cooperation in trade was established at a relatively early stage starting with certain specific sections, as developing countries we all have understandable difficulties in liberalising trade flows which might necessitate drastic changes in our trade regimes. But it should be possible to consider limited cooperation based on a regional system of trade preferences, cooperation among state trading agencies and trade related institutions and cooperation in the marketing of commodities of interest to countries of the region.

Indian leaders have been taking keen interest in SAARC summits on cooperative efforts. The theoretical efforts of India have always been encouraging irrespective of the practical result. It is important to discuss Indian head of states initiative during SAARC summits. Since the formation of SAARC India has taken keen interest to develop the idea of cooperation through an association. First meeting of foreign ministers SARC (South Asian Regional Cooperation) countries took place at New Delhi in August 1983, Mrs. Indira Gandhi in her inaugural address to the SAARC countries foreign ministers urged that the seven member countries must conduct their affairs so as to eliminate tension and promote greater peace and stability in the region and she also stressed against the attempts of external powers to influence our functioning.[38] After assuming the office as Prime Minister of India immediately after the assassination of Indira Gandhi, Rajiv Gandhi stressed that self-reliance and mutual cooperation in the affairs of SAARC should be encouraged. At the first summit of SAARC, held in Dhaka in December 1985 in his speech on the opening day Indian Prime Minister described the summit as a new dawn of people's movement for regional cooperation which poured the way for collective self-reliance in the fight against poverty, illiteracy, malnutrition and disease in the area.[39] India's Prime Minister Rajiv Gandhi admitted at the Bangaluru summit that "the SAARC summit has become an important fixture in our calendar for bilateral discussions and an exchange of views outside the conference premises." Rajiv Gandhi suggested that SAARC should meet once a year and not once in two years as planned. It was mentioned under Article III of the SAARC charter which mentioned that there will be one summit meeting in a year.[40] "In this direction Indian government was anxious to create a congenial atmosphere in a sub-continent prior to launching of SAARC."

In the second summit at Bangaluru, prime minister of India came out with a note on how to expand people to people contact. India wanted to open a frequent exchange of scholars, public figures, media and cultural programmes of artists etc. and it was in this direction that prime minister of India placed special emphasis on SAVE (SAARC Audio Visual Exchange) programme.[41] India has also tried to think about South Asian Common market. In the fourth summit of SAARC held in Islamabad in 1988, India expressed its frustration at the slow pace of cooperation in general and lack of cooperation in economic arena in particular. As neo-functionalism became successful in Europe, during the fifth summit, the then prime minister of India Chandra Shakher advocated functional approach and proposed for institutional cooperation within the South Asian region. This summit is also important for India in the sense that it afforded the opportunity for a direct dialogue between Indian and Pakistani prime ministers on Pakistani soil. This summit also suggested the preparation of a regional plan called 'SAARC 2000' to provide for basic needs for shelter, education and literacy. The summit took up environmental issues of the greenhouse effect for its study, and it also called for a war against narcotics. Chandra Shakher proposed that the tourist industry could be attracted from outside the region. Chandra Shakher urged SAARC to become a more vibrant organisation and virtually called for a new SAARC order free from the politics of confrontation.[42] The period 1989-90 saw some uncertainty in the process of Cooperation in SAARC. The all-round interest and enthusiasm that SAARC had been able to generate in the early years was marred by the uncertainty of Sri Lanka by not holding the SAARC summit at its prime time. Sri Lankan reluctance to hold the summit on account of Indo Sri Lanka bilateral issues put serious obstacles in the progress of SAARC. Sri Lanka raised the issue of the presence of Indian peace keeping force as a reason for its inability to hold the summit. The Indian peace keeping force (IPKF) despite having been sent on the invitation of the Sri Lankan government became a bone of contention. Eventually, the 1989 summit never took place and the fifth summit was then convened at Male in 1990. The Sri Lankan episode appears to have set a kind of precedent. The subsequent years have seen the cancellation or postponement of annual summits for relatively minor reasons.

In 1991, Indian government introduced the policy of economic reforms. Accordingly P.V. Narsimha Rao proposed "Collective Economic Security" system as the only alternative to fulfill the need for an effective safeguard for furthering development and strengthening economies of developing countries. He also remarked that the SAARC must adapt itself with vision and understanding to developments outside our region and emphasise on confidence among the people and governments to set in motion a benevolent cycle wherein cooperation strengthens confidence which in turn makes for closer cooperation.[43] He also proposed the member states to have a commercial exchanger among them at a faster pace with sustained commitment towards the free flow of trade besides policies encouraging cross investment within the economic region. He described SAPTA (South Asian preferential trading arrangement) proposed by Sri Lanka as development of historic importance for South Asia and exhorted the member states to take up the challenge of poverty and work for the upliftment of the people from the very base of pyramid.[44]

In the following two summits, India consistently recalled for the integration of SAARC economies and creation of a free market in order to enhance the range of dynamism and collective strength of the member states in a globally trading community. India wanted the South Asian states to adapt the successful approach of similar regional bodies in opening their doors to the free flow of goods, services, capital and manpower. India decided to closely examine the Sri Lanka's proposal to establish a SAARC preferential trading arrangement SAPTA South Asian preferential trade area by 1997. The agreement on SAARC preferential trading (SAPTA) was the first step in this direction. A preferential trading arrangement is the first, and perhaps the mildest form of regional economic integration. The agreement aimed at promoting and sustaining mutual trade and economic cooperation among the states of SAARC through the exchange of various concessions. The operationalisation of SAPTA in December 1995 and the subsequent three rounds of negotiations entailing tariff liberalisation have been the major developments in the regional trade liberalisation. The details of the tariff concessions offered by all SAARC countries shown in Tables 1 and 2 reveal that the largest number of concessions was offered by India.

Table 1: Number of products on which tariff concessions have been extended by SAARC member states in the three rounds of tariff negotiations under SAPTA

Countries	*First round*			*Second round*			*Third round*			*Grand total*
	LDCS	*All*	*Total*	*LDCS*	*All*	*Total*	*LDCS*	*all*	*Total*	
Bangladesh	1	11	12	11	215	226	143	338	481	719
Bhutan	7	4	11	10	37	47	101	23	124	182
India	62	44	106	514	390	904	1874	43	1919	2927
Maldives	0	17	17	3	2	5	0	368	368	390
Nepal	4	10	14	67	166	233	137	52	189	436
Pakistan	15	20	35	131	227	358	271	24	295	688
Sri Lanka	11	20	31	23	72	95	54	28	82	208
Total	**100**	**126**	**226**	**759**	**1109**	**1868**	**2580**	**876**	**3556**	**5550**

LDCS: low developed countries.

Source: SAARC secretariat cited in I. N. Mukherji (2004) "Towards a free trade area in south Asia: charting a feasible course for trade liberalisation with reference to India's role", RIS papers, No. 86, New Delhi, RIS.

Table 2: Depth of tariff concessions agreed by the SAARC member states in the three rounds of negotiations under SAPTA (%)

Countries	*First round*		*Second round*		*Third round*	
	For Ldcs	*For all*	*For Ldcs*	*For all*	*For Ldcs*	*For all*
Bangladesh	10	10	10	10	10.15	10
Bhutan	10, 13, 15	15	15	10	10, 18, 20	10
India	50, 100	10, 25, 30, 50, 90	25, 30	10, 15, 25, 40	50-100	10, 20
Maldives	7.5	7.5	15	10	5,10	5, 10
Nepal	10	10	15	10	10,15	10
Pakistan	15	10	15	10	30	20
Sri Lanka	10, 15	10, 20	10, 50, 60	10	10, 30, 50	10

Ldcs: low developed countries.

Source: SAARC secretariat cited in I.N. Mukherji (2004) "towards a free trade area in south Asia charting a feasible course for trade liberalisation with reference to India's role", RIS Discussion papers, No. 86, New Delhi, RIS (Research Information System).

An important aspect of Indian advocacy of South Asian cooperation is Gujral doctrine. It was a significant step in the direction of cooperation in South Asia favoured by I.K. Gujral (the then foreign minister of India). This doctrine comprises of five principles for regional cooperation. It covers economic cooperation, cooperation in security and non-interference and respect of each other's sovereignty and territory. In this direction during the tenth SAARC summit, India took some bold initiatives to enhance access to its market. Prime Minister of India namely, Atal Bihari Vajpayee announced that India would lift quantitative restrictions for SAARC countries with effect from August 1, 1998. This involved putting over 2000 products on open general license for SAARC countries. India's prime minister, A.B. Vajpayee also announced that the ceiling for overseas Indian investment in SAARC countries under fast track procedures would be increased from $8 million to $15 million. India was also willing to consider bilateral free trade agreements with those countries which were interested in moving further. In the wake of military coup in Pakistan in October in 1999, India refused to attend the next summit. This was appreciated as an indication of India's commitment to encourage a greater flow of Indian investment in its immediate neighbourhood.[45] At the twelfth summit of SAARC, India's main concern was combating terrorism and to remove the poverty. The then prime minister of India Atal Bihari Vajpayee mooted a proposal to give $ 100 million to SAARC for combating poverty. He suggested that India, Pakistan and Bangladesh should jointly celebrate the 150th anniversary of 1857 uprising against colonial rule because our forefathers fought against a common colonial oppressor.[46]

In the next summit in Dhaka Prime Minister of India, Dr. Manmohan Singh laid stress on a larger role for India in South Asian region in a year. He particularly advocated energy cooperation. India proposed in the ministerial meeting that it was ready to open South Asian skies improving connectivity among SAARC countries as a means to create better platform for regional cooperation. India also welcomed to induct Afghanistan as member of the SAARC.[47] Indian proposal for establishment of a South Asian University for the whole region was encouraging. India also proposed to establish a South Asia food security store to meet the emergency needs in case of any food shortage in any part of the region. Along with it Indian prime minister offered South Asian car rally which would symbolise regional identity and draw attention to the urgent need to improve transport infrastructure in member nations. South Asian car rally which began successfully from Cox's Bazaar (Bangladesh) on March 15, 2007 to bring the SAARC nations to more close ties would symbolise regional identification and draw attention to the urgent need to improve transport infrastructure in member countries. Dr. Manmohan Singh, the Prime Minister of India, has termed the Asian Economic Community as constituting 'an arc of advantage' in terms of prosperity, stability and closer economic integration where there would be large-scale movement of people, capital, labour, ideas and creativity.[48] In the fourteenth SAARC summit India allowed duty free access to goods to its vast market for the least developed members of SAARC. India also announced unilateral liberalisation of visas for students, teachers, professors, journalists and patients from SAARC countries. In this meeting establishment of South Asian University in New Delhi is also approved. India was the chair of the SAARC from 2007-2008. In the fifteenth summit held in Colombo in 2008 trade and investment linkages were further consolidated. In this summit India expressed its deep concern over the serious threat posed by terrorism to peace, stability and security of the nation. In the sixteenth summit of SAARC held in Thimpu, 2010 Indian Prime Minister Manmohan Singh described the accomplishment of SAARC as "half empty glass".[49] The deadlock over the composite dialogue after the Mumbai terrorist attack in 2008 between India and Pakistan also came to an end. India also announced setting up of a fund that would help South Asia effectively meet urgent adaptation and capacity building needs posed by climate change. India called to double the intra SAARC flow of tourists in the next five years, India recalled for energy cooperation and South Asian development fund. The 17th SAARC summit was held at Maldives capital of Male on November 10-11, 2011. In this summit Indian Prime Minister Manmohan Singh laid emphasis on trade which should flourish among SAARC countries with very low tariffs among themselves so as to ensure smooth trade between the member countries without any hurdle imposed through high custom duties in this era of liberalisation.

Notes

1. Gujral, I. K. (2001), *"India and Her Neighbours*", *Mainstream*, New Delhi.
2. Ehsaas, Farhat (2003), *"SAARC: Relevance's in New World Order"*, References Press, New Delhi, p. 1.
3. Mehotra, L.L. *et.al,* (1995), "*SAARC 2000 and Beyond",* Omega Publishers, New Delhi, p.14.
4. Preamble of the United Nations Charter.
5. Shukla, Vijay (1996), "New Frontiers of SAARC," *India Quarterly*, Vol. 2, No.1-2, New Delhi, p. 105.
6. C. Kishore Dash (1996), "The Political Economy of Regional Cooperation in South Asia", *Pacific Affairs*, Vol. 69, No. 2, summer, pp. 117-118.
7. Naqash, Nasir Ahmad, (1994), "*SAARC: Challenges and Opportunities*, Ashish Publishing House, New Delhi, n 18, p. 5.
8. C. Kishore Dash (1996), "The Political Economy of Regional Cooperation in South Asia", *Pacific Affairs*, summer, Vol. 69. No. 2, p. 20.
9. *Ibid.*
10. K.B. Lall and *et al.* (1993), "*The European Community and SAARC,*" Radiant Publishers, New Delhi, p. 31.
11. Four meetings at Foreign Secretary level were held on (I) April 21-23, 1981, Colombo (II) November 2-4, 1981, Kathmandu, (III) August 7-8, 1982, Islamabad and (IV) March 28-30, 1983, Dhaka.
12. Grover, Verinder (1997), "*Encyclopedia of SAARC Nations",* Vol. 1, Deep and Deep Publications, New Delhi, pp. 635-637.
13. SAARC Charter at http//www.sec.org
14. Article II of SAARC Charter
15. Article III of SAARC Charter
16. *Ibid.*
17. Article IV of SAARC Charter
18. Article V of SAARC Charter
19. Article VI of SAARC Charter
20. Article VII of SAARC charter
21. Chandra, Prakash and Arora, Prem (2008), *International Politics*; Cosmos Bookhive, New Delhi, p. 357.
22. Gupta, Sisir (1964), "*India and Regional Integration in Asia",* Asia Publishing House, New Delhi, pp. 28-29.
23. *Ibid.*
24. Sharma, Suman, "India and the Origin of SAARC", *World Focus*, Joshi Colony, New Delhi, Vol. 31, No. 7, July, 2010, pp. 254-255.
25. The Egyptian political party that was instrumental in gaining the freedom for Egypt from Great Britain.

26. Sharma, Suman, "India and the Origin of SAARC", *World Focus*, Joshi Colony, New Delhi, Vol.31, no.7, July, 2010, pp. 254-255.
27. Bradnock, Robert W. (1990), *India's Foreign Policy Since 1971*, London, p. 1.
28. Muni, S.D. and Muni Anuradha (1984), "*Regional Cooperation in South Asia*," National Publishing House, New Delhi, pp. 29-31.
29. *"From SARC to SAARC: Milestones in the Evolution of Regional Cooperation in South Asia*" (1980-88), Volume I, SAARC Secretariat, Kathmandu, 1988, p. 2.
30. *Ibid*. p. 7.
31. Gupta, Sisir (1964), "*India and Regional Integration in Asia",* Asia Publishing House, New Delhi, pp. 25-26.
32. Sharma, Suman, "India and the Origin of SAARC", *World Focus*, Joshi Colony, New Delhi, Vol. 31, No. 7, July, 2010, pp. 254-255.
33. *Ibid*.
34. *Ibid*.
35. *Ibid*.
36. Bhatty, Maqbool Ahmad, (1991-92), "The Future of SAARC," *Regional Studies*, Vol.10, no.1. Winter, pp. 95-96.
37. Ayer, Mani Shankar (1998), *Rajiv Gandhi's Foreign Policy*, Vol. 3, New Delhi, UBS Publishers, p.43.
38. *Ibid*. p. 184.
39. *Ibid*. p. 186.
40. *Ibid*. p. 179.
41. Mohala, Vandana, (1998), "*SAARC and Superpower*," Deep and Deep Publications, New Delhi, pp. 133-138.
42. Upreti, B.C. (2008), *SAARC: Dynamics of Regional Cooperation in South Asia*, Vol. 1, Kalinga Publication, New Delhi, p. 156.
43. Mohala, Vandana (1998), *"SAARC and Superpower*," Deep and Deep Publications, New Delhi, p. 146.
44. *Ibid*. p. 167.
45. *India's Foreign Relations*, 1998-99, http://www. India embassy.org/policy/foreign policy/fp_1999/saarc
46. http://www. India embassy.org/policy/foreign policy/fp_1999/saarc
47. *The Tribune*, January 6, 2004.
48. *"SAARC 2015 Expanding Horizons and Forging Cooperation in a Resurgent Asia"* the New Delhi *Statement on SAARC 2015 and Asian Resurgence,* Friedrich-Ebert-Stiftung India Office, New Delhi, p. 5.
49. *Civil Service Chronicle*, May, 2010.

Chapter - 3

India as a Regional Hegemon and its Impact on the Development of SAARC

India as Core of the Region

India's location at the base of the continental Asia and at the top of Indian Ocean gives it a vantage position in relation to both Central Asia and the Indian Ocean Region (IOR). Additionally, India's size, strategic location, trade links and exclusive economic zone (EEZ) links its security environment directly with the extended neighbourhood, particularly with neighbouring countries and the regions of Central Asia, South East Asia, the Gulf and the Indian Ocean. These strategic factors impose an increasingly larger responsibility on India.[1] For all its near billion population, to its potential booming economy and its admirably efficient army, India always seems to be held back by its fragile sense of national identity, the geographic isolation of the Indian subcontinent between mountain and sea, the inward looking nature of the Hindu religion-becoming the sort of country that strides confidently onto the world stage.[2]

As the modern avatar of an ancient civilisation and heir to the British Empire's pre-eminence, India's overriding national security goal is to establish its rightful place in the emerging world order.[3] While the main thrust of Indian foreign policy has been consistent since independence, India is "on the verge of multiple breakthroughs."[4] Even if this assessment proves premature, New Delhi has successfully maintained the general contours of its grand strategy amidst several changes of governance since 1991 and is unlikely to make major alterations in the near future.

India is on the world's stage as the first large, economically powerful, culturally vibrant, multi-ethnic, multi-religious democracy. India has the potential to become leading member of the political West and to play a key role politically in the coming decades. Whether it will and how soon depends on the readiness of the western powers to engage India on its own terms.[5] However, India does not enjoy a benign security environment and is increasingly challenged by states that have adversarial ties with New Delhi reflected through the baggage of history as well an unsettled boundary and territorial issues. Further the issue of states with weak state institutions along its borders compounds the problems for India.

In practical terms, securing India's great power goals impose two strategic requirements. The first is a sustained economic growth rate[6] which largely depends on uninterrupted access to foreign sources of energy. Given the small contribution that nuclear power currently makes and the long lead time involved in its significant expansion, the oil and natural gas components of energy security occupy a silent position in India's strategic thinking. India's geographic position along the sea lanes' connecting the Persian Gulf with Asia's other growing economies reinforces India's potential to be a security provider along this crucial route. The second strategic need is to secure access to energy resources and unhindered foreign trade, which will have an impact on the direction of development. This brings out the importance of the extended South Asia region which includes the littoral states of the Indian Ocean.[7] India today belongs to a club of nations that has developed nuclear powered submarines, launched remote sensing satellites (with the ability to map the earth's resources from outer space) and launched intermediate range ballistic missiles. Its launching of the polar satellite launch vehicle in October 1994 was impressive.

The enabling and constraining capabilities of India with regard to promoting regional cooperation in South Asia had been discussed even before the conceptual journey of the South Asian Association for Regional Cooperation (SAARC) began in 1983. India occupies a unique position in the South Asian Region. By virtue of its size, location and economic potential India assumes a natural leadership role in the region. But the over-bearing presence of a neighbour with aspirations for global leadership has also been a source of apprehensions for the other South Asian countries. Consequently, cooperative efforts of the South Asian countries are hijacked by the dilemma of comprehending India's perceived and actual role as a stepping stone or a stumbling block for the regional efforts. India claims a leadership position for herself, while her South Asian neighbours accuse her of exercising hegemony. India's neighbours feel themselves threatened by the bigger centre of power and accuse it of hegemonistic designs.[8] India represents a menacing and aggressive monster that sends nervous tremors through the region every time it shrugs even in statistical terms. Its military strength in comparison to rest is awesome. Indian preponderance is clearly recognised by the superpowers and it's widely believed proximity to the Soviet Union in geographical terms gives India an added air of invisible menace. India shares borders with all South Asian countries, making it the vital physical link in the region. These contrasting approaches to the issue of strategic consensus in South Asia to the building of a regional security structure in the subcontinent lie at the root of most of the political problems that bedevil India's relations with its smaller South Asian neighbours. They also complicate and are complicated by, India's uneasy relations with its largest neighbour China. Thus, even if the current relaxed state of relations between Moscow and Washington becomes a long-term trend, this will not necessarily lead to a lessening of tensions in South Asia for India.

Lakshman Kadirgamar a leading writer of Sri Lanka on south Asian affairs has used the analogy of a wheel to depict centrality of India in South Asian affairs. According to him, at the hub of the wheel lies regionally preponderant India. Radiating as spokes are India's neighbours with each of whom India shares land or maritime boundaries, but no two others are thus joined without at the same time touching India also. Binding those spokes to that hub are the physical barriers.[9] The South Asian nations in particular and global powers in general regard India to assume additional responsibility for ensuing regional development and cohesion. In the words of Jayewardene "India was expected to create the confidence among the countries so necessary to make a beginning, and was referred to as the "key to the development and progress of SAARC".[10]

India's responsibility in shaping and directing the cooperation drive was recognised by extra-regional powers. The size and position of India give it a special role of leadership in South Asian and world affairs.[11] The overall changes in international politics after the end of the Cold War further reinforced the primacy of the India factor in the region. According to Mohammed Ayoub, the changing nature of Superpower relations has opened up prospects for regionally preeminent powers to adopt more overt managerial roles in their respective regions.[12]

India's Response to the New International Order

India like many other developing countries responded to the post cold war developments in the arena of international politics. It tried to adjust to the situation and accordingly attempted to rearrange its foreign policy priorities both at the global and regional levels. India's adherence to the policy of nonalignment, peace, friendship and stability continued. Yet it was necessary to bring about certain changes in India's foreign policy in response to the new emerging world order.[13] In fact, it was not possible for any country to remain isolated from the growing emphasis on globalisation and privatisation on the one hand and the reshaping and realigning of global political and strategic forces from the other.

In fact, these changes posed new challenges for India's foreign policy and the disintegration of the Soviet Union particularly necessitated the recasting of its foreign policy priorities. India realised that in the changed circumstances regional issues had become more important and it was necessary to build strong ties at the regional level. In response to the changing world scenario and the need for a fresh look at India's foreign policy India's Prime Minister Narasimha Roa said in parliament on December 20, 1991 that his government was prepared to adopt itself to the changing international environment.[14] India was conscious of the need to structure a regional and international order based on harmony, consensus and willingness to strive for peace, stability and development.

It became essential for Indian foreign policy to take into account,

(i) India's security and territorial integrity;

(ii) The economic well being of the people which required keeping pace with the external economic environment;

(iii) Stability and peace in the region.

In the context of India's foreign policy towards its neighbouring countries certain aspects acquired significance. Firstly, there was a pressing need to recast India's approach and envisaging its role with regard to the politico-strategic issues in the context of two major developments, the disintegration of its dependable all the Soviet Union and the lessening of possibilities of big power involvement in regional affairs. Secondly, in the context of the globalisation and privatisation of economies, regional cohesion and the activation of regional economic cooperation became necessary in order to cope with the changes. Thirdly, there was an increasing need for greater and more sustained efforts to promote better bilateral relations with the neighbouring countries, which could help develop a congenial atmosphere for financial investment, joint ventures, expansion of market facilities, transfer of technology, liberalisation of trade regimes, etc. at the regional level. Fourthly, India began to realise that the growth of democratic institutions in the neighbouring countries could be an asset for the development of healthy bilateral relations and regional solidarity. Fifthly, India's response to end initiatives in the emerging world order has an inevitable impact on and significance for its South Asian neighbours. And lastly, India's concern in reshaping its foreign policy, in accordance with changing priorities in regional affairs, was induced not only by the changes at the global level but also by the changes in the neighbouring countries themselves.[15]

Shift in Regional Scenario

The changes taking place at the global level influenced the countries of South Asia too. It appeared that competitive polity was gradually taking the place of controlled regimes. In Pakistan, with the death of President Zia Ul Haq in 1988 the army realised that it could no longer prevent the advent of democracy and for a few following years, the country moved back to the path of democracy. In Sri Lanka, presidential elections took place in 1989. In Bangladesh, democracy came into operation with the 1988 general elections. In Nepal, the 1990 democratic movement succeeded in establishing democracy.[16]

Along with the democratisation of polity in the neighbouring countries India also witnessed political changes at home. The formation of non-Congress governments not only marked a change of ruling party but also indicated the beginning of weak governments and weak political leadership in India. These changes impacted on India's relations with its South Asian neighbours. India had strained relations with Pakistan over the issue of Siachen, nuclear tests, Kashmir and cross-border terrorist activities, with Nepal over the issues of arms purchase from China and the renewal of trade and transit treatises; with Sri Lanka over the issue of withdrawal of the Indian peace keeping force (IPKF) and with Bangladesh over the issue of sharing the Ganga waters, illegal migrants and arms supply from China. With the change in party and leadership in India a change in the attitudes of the government was obvious. It can be concluded that the post cold war period was marked by significant changes which had a bearing on the pattern of international relations. Individual countries had to reshape their foreign policies in accordance with the changing international scenario. It called for an emphasis on building strong regional ties by improving relations with immediate neighbours. India's preparedness to accept these developments and recast its foreign policy priorities helped the foreign policy orientation of its neighbouring countries.[17] However it may be pointed about here that the new emerging world order could not lead to the disappearance of conflicts, it could only create certain opportunities which could help minimise conflicts and develop good neighbourly relationships.

Initiatives and Constraints

After 1990s India began to take initiatives to improve relations with its neighbouring countries. India's relations with Bhutan had been cordial and continued to be the same despite the emergence of ethnic conflict in Bhutan and strained Bhutan-Nepal relations. India is refrained from commenting on the issue and did not allow its relations with Bhutan to disturb.[18] With Nepal, a process of normalisation of relations started with the signing of the accord in June 1990, restoring the prior status of April 1987. The revision of trade and transit treatises, which had become a note of discord between the two countries during 1987-88, further strengthened their relationship. India agreed to provide economic concessions to Nepal in order to encourage trade. India and Nepal also developed understanding on the issue of mutually beneficial utilisation of the Mahakali River. For Sri Lanka, India's withdrawal of the IPKF in 1990 was a great relief. It indeed paved the way for the improvement of relation between the two countries. In 1991, the two countries agreed to the setting up of a joint commission to provide an institutional framework to their bilateral relations. India's relations with Bangladesh remained unstable during 1975-90.[19] The Khalida Zia government which came to power in February 1991 could not make much headway except in resolving the Tin Bigha issue.

India's relation with Pakistan however remained same as they were in the past vitiated by a hostility that was basically the legacy of history.[20] The suitable government created after 1990 did not help much in removing mutual distrust and suspicion. India did try to improve trade relations and encourage cultural relations with Pakistan, but issues concerning Kashmir, cross-border terrorist activities, nuclear development, narcotic and drug trafficking, etc. remained unresolved.

On the whole, India's South Asia policy lacked a clear and broad perspective. All efforts towards building bridges and the confidence building measures proved to be mere rhetoric and were confined to strengthening public relations.[21]

India as a Regional Power: Policies and Perception

Hegemony is the privileged exercise of power in complete disregard to the interests of other states. Indian policies with regard to the liberation movement in Bangladesh in 1971, the ethnic crisis in Sri Lanka in 1987 and the attempted military coup in Maldives in 1988 are cited as illustrations of India's hegemonic authority in region. Even diplomatic statements, like the Indian Government's comment on the deteriorating conditions in Baluchistan and also the advice for Pakistan Government to exercise restraint has been interpreted as interference by India.

India has defended its Bangladesh policy on the grounds that India intervened only after her requests to the United Nations to act against Pakistan failed to yield results. "The Guardian"[22] had described the Pakistani troop's atrocities as an arrogant crime against humanity and human aspirations.[23] Given the compulsions of national security coupled with the humanitarian crisis in East Pakistan, India sought to provide military assistance that led to the emergence of Bangladesh. The military involvement by India is further defended by referring to the request for the same by Sheikh Mujibur Rahman, the founding father of Bangladesh. Despite all justifications, the role played by India in the emergence of Bangladesh is viewed even today as a vindication of the regional apprehensions. The most important result of the 1971 crisis on regional perceptions has been the demonstrated ability of India to alter the geo-political landscape of South Asia. India is accused of using the Indo-Sri Lanka Accord of 1987 to assert its military potential in the region. The accord allowed India's diplomatic involvement in resolving the confrontation between the Tamil and Sinhalese in Sri Lanka and the option of military assistance was expected to be contingency clause, which few expected would be utilised. The deterioration of the security situation in Sri Lanka and the fickle policies of President Premadasa forced India to get militarily involved in the Island politics. The professions of caution and restraint provided by India have done little to address the regional fear psychosis generated in response to the episode.[24] The fallout of India's gaffe in Sri Lanka was so immense that even the ministerial level meetings for launching SAARC were adversely affected. In November 1988 the Indian military in response to a request by the de jure government of Maldives helped to crush an attempted coup on the island. The Maldives episode, as an individual case study would have perhaps not invited much attention, but the fact that it took place barely a year after India's military involvement in Sri Lanka sought to reinforce the negative perceptions about India. The importance of the Maldivian episode lies in the kind of the reinforcements it provided for the apprehensions about India's politico-military clout in South Asia.

India's relations with her South Asian neighbours are characterised by numerous bilateral contentions. India favours a bilateral dialogue for addressing these concerns, while the neighbours demand a multilateral regional approach. India fears that the neighbours would gang-up against her and demand unrealistic concessions in a multi-lateral scenario, while the neighbours suspect that India seeks to take undue advantage of the weak bargaining capacity of each state in a bilateral dialogue. Neighbours view Indian bilateralism as an instrument of coercive diplomacy, while India considers the demand of multilateralism as an unnecessary burden of the nascent and fragile process of SAARC. Moreover, India unlike Indonesia has not shown any serious interest in the organisation as it prefers to cooperate with smaller neighbours only on a bilateral basis. Inter-state interaction is a multi-dimensional process involving bilateral, regional and other forms of multilateral relations. In South Asia, the disagreement over the most preferred strategy emerges from the perceptual divergence among regional states. The psychological predispositions have come to be so shaped that any reference of bilateralism translates into possibilities of Indian hegemony and any assertion of multilateralism is deciphered as a pressure generating tactic, irrespective of the actual merits of either approaches. The most obvious example cited as a justification of India's hegemonic aspirations is the Indira Doctrine. The Indira doctrine was an implicit foreign and security policy response to the newly regional security environment in South Asia. The essence of the Indira doctrine was India's claim for hegemonic status in the region and represented a tough and uncompromising attitude toward neighbours, large and small.[25]

Two principles of Indira doctrine are

(i) No foreign power should be involved in the South Asian Region;

(ii) The involvement of any foreign power that does not recognise India's predominance in the region would be treated as an inimical to India's interest.

Indira doctrine emphasised that no South Asia nation should ask for outside assistance from any country, if a South Asian nation genuinely needs external assistance, it should seek it from India. A failure to do so will be considered anti-India.[26] From this perspective Indian concerns are predominant in South Asia, especially over those of external powers who must not be allowed to exploit crises to enhance their own positions in the region. By implication, any attempt by another South Asian nation to invite such outside intervention will be considered hostile to India and grounds for Indian retaliation. In short, Indian security policy in South Asia is based on denying external powers a regional foothold with military force if necessary. Indira doctrine is India's Monroe doctrine as its strategic predominance in the region is asserted by denying external powers a regional foothold. Indira Gandhi's enunciation of this doctrine is a direct reflection of the systemic, domestic and individual level influences in her foreign policy strategies.

Rajiv Gandhi then Prime Minister of India formulated a grand strategy following Indira doctrine. Rajiv Gandhi followed the inherited, the restive domestic and neighbourhood region where threat perceptions were emanating from several quarters. India and Pakistan had fought two full scale wars – first in 1965 and then in 1971 when Pakistan lost its eastern territory, Sino-Pakistan friendship began in an upward swing after India's nuclear tests in 1974, the problem of Sikh separatism led to the assassination of Indira Gandhi, the ethnic Tamil factor in India Sri Lanka relations troubled India's military engagement with Sri Lanka, the threat of Islamic fundamentalism coming to power in Afghanistan as soon as Soviet forces withdraw and Nepal's decision to procure arms from China aggravated India's security doctrines.

Rajiv Gandhi responded to the threats of insecurities with strong military and diplomatic policies. His bilateral policies towards Pakistan, Nepal, Bhutan and Sri Lanka and his grand strategic framework in the neighbourhood remained in tune with Indira doctrine. In 1986, Rajiv supported Indian military's plan and completely personalised his decision-making in handling the crisis.[27] He flexed India's hegemonic muscle against Nepal when it was determined to seek an independent path from India. India imposed an economic blockade on Nepal that resulted in serious economic distress and shortage of vital goods in Nepal.[28] The Indo-Sri Lanka peace accord was signed in June, 1987 and the IPKF (Indian peace keeping force) was sent to Sri Lanka for guaranteeing and enforcing cessations of hostilities in Sri Lanka. Besides India's engagement in Maldives was one of the success stories of India's military missions in the neighbourhood. An attempt to overthrow Maldivian president Maumoon Abdul Gayoom in November 1988 was organised by a wealthy businessman Abdullah Luthufi. Such extensive military engagements in the neighbourhood underscored India's desire to establish regional supremacy.

The origins of the Doctrine are traced to the Sri Lankan crisis of 1988 and laid down that India would consider the presence or influence of an external power in the region as adverse to its interests. India's justification for the policy was an attempt to protect the region from the adverse effects of the Cold War, but the neighbours viewed it as a policy to abolish any challenge to India's regional position. In the recent years India has not only allowed but in fact aligned with extra-regional powers to address regional issues, but the regional perceptions fail to take notice of these developments. There was 'outstanding cooperation' between US and Indian ambassadors to try and get Nepal back to multiparty democracy.[29]

The Gujral Doctrine, India's policy of providing unilateral concessions to South Asian neighbours without seeking reciprocity proved to be too mild in the face of the impregnable perceptual framework of India's neighbours. Altaf Gauhar, leading Pakistani columnist commented that, "The Gujral Doctrine is not a doctrine of good neighbourly relations but a Bharti Plan to seize the neighbour peacefully."[30] Regional economic cooperation is viewed by regional states as a mechanism of ensuring the economic empowerment of India at the expense of her South Asian neighbours.

The South Asian countries were not enthusiastic about South Asian Preferential Trading Agreement (SAPTA) because they felt that the impact of their unfavourable trade balance with India would be accentuated if liberalisation is encouraged in regional context. Countries in the region also fear that if market forces are allowed to guide the intraregional trade India would emerge as the dominating factor leading to the political dependence of these states on India.

Sadar Assef Ali, Foreign Minister of Pakistan and Mustafiz ur Rahman, Foreign Minister of Bangladesh clearly stated that despite their obligations under the Marrakesh and WTO (World Trade Organisation) arrangement they would not be able to respond to India under those obligations till political issues like Kashmir and Farakka are resolved.[31] The fear rather than the existence of Indian hegemon makes the South Asian states apathetic to pursuing mutually beneficial economic policies. The regional hegemonic doctrine proposed by BJP was in response to the threats regional security environment in South Asia experienced. The essence of the BJP's regional doctrine was asserting India's primacy in the region by implicitly forcing deference from all its neighbours.

Contrary to regional expectations, expansion of economic relations with India has benefited the regional economies and India has granted numerous economic concessions. In the case of Nepal, for instance, the constraint of the value-added component imposed on Nepali products for duty-free entry into the Indian market was reduced from 80 per cent to 50 per cent, and now even this has been completely removed. In relation to Bangladesh and Sri Lanka, India agrees in principle to reduce their adverse trade balances but the modalities have still to be worked out.[32] Following the Gujral Doctrine, India announced at the 1997 Male Summit to unilaterally withdraw restraints to entry to India of all exports from within the South Asian region, including Pakistan. Indian companies had invested US$ 83 million in 140 ventures till 1999 in four SMCs (Stock Market Companies). In addition Indian companies have extended US$ 3.5 million worth of loans and credits and guarantees worth $ 16.5 million to their affiliates in the SAARC region.[33] As a major positive development for regional cooperation India's preferential imports as compared to 1996 became more diversified in 2000.[34] India already has a free trading arrangement with Bhutan, Nepal and Sri Lanka and negotiations are underway for a free trade agreement with Bangladesh. India has adopted a preferential policy towards investment in SAARC countries. A fast track channel for processing investment proposals has been created to expedite projects. The ceiling for processing investments under the fast track channel had been increased from an initial US$ 4 million to US$ 15 million and further to US$ 30 million in May 1999, in case of member countries of SAARC other than Nepal and Bhutan.[35]

According to Pervaiz Iqbal Cheema, the most important impediment on the road to collective self reliance is not the incumbent asymmetry and the overwhelming stature of India but how other members perceive India's intentions with reservations and apprehensions.[36] India's regional policies can be criticised for being short-sighted and errant on certain counts, but the perceptions of regional states have interpreted these as policies of domination. This does not imply that India has never pursued dominating policies but these cannot be likened to the designs of imperial hegemony. India's policies of demanding certain concessions can be classified as arrogant but not outright hegemonic. Realisation of these diplomatic and perceptual limitations by the South Asian states could put an end to the blame-game being played out in the region.

Manmohan Singh Prime Minister of India believes that India's new regionalism must be rooted in self interest. It is not that India is unaware of the SAARC organisation's many weaknesses. Nor does it delude itself that SAARC can be made into a dynamic organisation overnight. What New Delhi believes is that unilateral initiative can in fact accelerate the inevitable trends towards reshaping of the region.[37] The present emphasis on deepening regional integration is rooted in both political realism and economic pragmatism.

India's Trade with SAARC Members

South Asia's intraregional trade as a share of total trade remained below five per cent in the 1980s and 1990s and continues to be around the same level at present. At a broad level, the available data of the major South Asian countries indicate that industrial countries continue to assume a major share of the region's trade, while developing countries outside South Asia have been the second most important group, although their importance has been steadily diminishing.

Though the imports from SAARC increased steadily during the period and have quadrupled, it remained around one per cent of India's global imports since 1998-99.

Despite the fact that most of its neighbours are import dependent, India's trade with its neighbouring countries has not been very impressive, both in terms of volume and as a percentage of its global trade. India's intra SAARC trade is approximately 2.6 per cent of its total trade, with India's exports to SAARC countries constituting roughly 5 per cent of its total exports and India's imports from the SAARC countries constituting only 0.9 per cent of its total imports.

Even though the trade volume has increased in the recent years, it is much below the true potential.

Given the size of the Indian economy and its geographical positioning at the centre of the region, the success of trade initiatives taken in the SAARC region greatly depends on India and therefore India needs to play a greater role in ensuring that the goals of SAFTA are achieved. However, it is important to note that the official accounts of South Asia's international trade statistics are flawed by the high incidence of informal trade between India and its neighbours. The data merely captures the formal trade which takes place among the neighbouring countries. Studies have shown that huge informal trade takes place through the bordering countries for instance; the informal trade between India and Pakistan was estimated to be US$ 1bn for the year 2004-2005.[38]

According to the World Bank Report on 'India Bangladesh Trade, Trade Policies and Potential Free Trade Agreement', very approximate estimates based on surveys in Bangladesh during 2002, total smuggled exports from India to Bangladesh have been around US$ 500 mn, about 42 per cent of Bangladesh's recorded imports from India in 2002-03, or about 30 percent of total imports. Most of the smuggled imports came by the land border. Similarly, informal exports to India from Bangladesh, Nepal and Sri Lanka are also relatively high though they comprise a sizable share of third country goods. These national estimates of informal trade based on a sample survey of key locations may have high error margins and may not be fully reliable.[39] However, the available information on the informal trade does not significantly alter the pattern of intraregional trade. India is not likely to change its directions.

Indian hegemonism will continue to plague the region because it believes that its place as the overlord of the Indian Ocean is secure with the new Western alliances. But the small nations have the power collectively to tie up India as Lilliputians tied down Gulliver. Those familiar with Gulliver's Travels will not forget how Gulliver the giant in the land of pygmies put out the fire in the Queen's house and just opened his fly and eased his bladder.[40] The Lilliputian neighbours are sick of the smell of Indian urine. The Indians may enjoy the urine of even the cow and may find some medicinal properties in it. But the SAARC must consider ways to put an end to Indian hegemony covered in pompous piety. They must decide whether they will drown in a deluge flowing from a Gulliverian bladder or jointly plot and plan to tie down the Gulliver. Indian bladder politics, if it goes on, will degrade small nations that believe in preserving their dignity and self-respect.[41]

Challenges to Indian Hegemony in South Asia: China and Pakistan:

Chinese Response to India's Hegemony Role in South Asia

The improving relations between New Delhi and Washington offer some hope of easing external constraints on India's regional role, but China continues to remain a major worry for India. Beijing's intrusive role in South Asia has created major problems for India as far as the management of interstate relations in the region are concerned. Since the late 1950s India's relations with China only overtly nuclear state in South Asia have been antagonistic in character. There has been some improvement over the years as seen in the official visit by Prime Minister Rajiv Gandhi to Beijing in December 1988.

The basic problems between the two countries, including the disputed border and the asymmetry in their nuclear capabilities continue to haunt their relationship. It was not until 1959 when Tibet's Dalai Lama fled to India and border clashes between India and China escalated and with this Sino-Indian differences came out into the open.

As Sino-Indian relations deteriorated from the late 1950s onward Beijing began to side both politically and militarily with Pakistan in its disputes with New Delhi. In response to this two-front threat from China and Pakistan, India's defence expenditures escalated beginning in the early 1960's. This generated increased pressure on the Indian economy. In the wake of the 1959 uprising in Tibet against Chinese control and the Indian decision to give refuge to the Dalai Lama, Beijing began to encourage anti-Indian sentiments in the sub-Himalayan monarchies of Nepal, Bhutan and Sikkim. China also supplied training and weapons to various tribal insurgencies in North-Eastern India.[42]

The Sino-Indian border war of October-November 1962, which ended in a humiliating defeat for India, can be considered the military high point of the adversarial relationship between India and China.

The more perceptive members of India's foreign policy and defence community have been firmly of the opinion since the 1960s that Pakistan posed an immediate, short-term threat to Indian security, the long-term and far more serious threat came from China. They believe that while conflict with Pakistan is a more likely possibility than war with China in the short run, Pakistan's capacity to hurt India's vital interests is limited by the sheer asymmetry in indigenous resources that can be mobilised by the two countries in times of conflict. China is a different kind of power altogether. It has in the past demonstrated its military superiority over India as in the border war of 1962, and is more than a match for India in demographic terms. China has also built an impressive industrial and technological infrastructure, which is reflected not only in its conventional military power but also in its capacity to produce and deliver sophisticated nuclear weapons.

In fact, India's strivings for nuclear capability were related more to the asymmetrical nature of the Sino-Indian nuclear equation than to the Pakistan factor or to the double standard of the Nuclear Non-Proliferation Treaty. While it may address Pakistan's main security concern, it does not even begin to address India's major security problem in the sphere of nuclear weaponry.

The imbalance in nuclear capability between India and China has also created a negative impact on the Sino-Indian border problem from New Delhi's point of view. It is difficult for the two parties to find a solution that would be acceptable to both governments as well as to the Indian public. New Delhi's main anxiety seems to be that once Beijing is relieved of the political and military uncertainty, it may adopt a more aggressive posture in its own neighbourhood in South and Southeast Asia. New Delhi is particularly worried that if Chinese influence in Southeast Asia increases, this will embolden China to challenge India on its doorsteps in South Asia in the sub-Himalayan Kingdom's of Nepal and Bhutan. New Delhi has viewed the escalation of China's rhetoric since 1987 regarding disputed territories in northeastern India as part of a Chinese strategy that does not rule out renewed confrontation with India.

Indian displeasure with Nepal was ostensibly triggered by a dispute related to the renegotiation of a trade and transit agreement that expired in March 1989. It was in fact a manifestation of Indian anxiety that Kathmandu was deliberately downgrading its relations with India in favour of China. While tension between India and Nepal over China's role in the sub-Himalayan kingdom can be traced back to the 1960's, it was a series of Nepalese actions in 1988 that precipitated India's tough line.

Pakistan Response to India's Hegemonic Role in South Asia

Pakistan has been able to exploit the "China card" and remains the strongest challenge to the managerial role that India aspires to play in South Asia. The dispute over Kashmir and the bloodshed that accompanied the division of the British Indian Empire have contributed to the hostile nature of India-Pakistan relations. But they are not the primary causes of today's antagonistic relationship.

The major factor bedeviling India-Pakistan relations is more fundamental and relates to the lack of congruence between the two countries' political elites in terms of how they view their respective roles in South Asia. Pakistan's ability to borrow power from abroad-principally from the United States and China- has allowed it to maintain a position of near parity with India in military terms. Thus, an atmosphere of tension persists in the subcontinent, where the fear of another India-Pakistan conflict lurks just beneath the surface. It also allows the military to "legitimately" appropriate a large segment of national revenues for expenditure on weapons and military perks.[43]

India's political elites prefer to deal with civilian leaders in Pakistan feeling they have more in common with them than with Pakistani generals because the two wars with Pakistan occurred during military leadership in Pakistan. This is the major reason why India-Pakistan relations have lost much of their hostile edge since Benazir Bhutto's election as prime minister of Pakistan in 1988. A similar trend was visible from 1972 to 1977 during her father's rule despite the elder Bhutto's virulently anti-Indian past.[44]

Pakistan was created in 1947 under the assumption that Indian Muslims needed a homeland of their own. That home-land was to consist of the Muslim majority provinces of British India. Yet the movement for Pakistan was primarily conducted in the Muslim minority provinces, where the Muslim elite were fearful of Hindu domination in an independent India.

The India-Pakistan relationship is a classic example of the "security dilemma," in which an increase in one state's capabilities enhances the vulnerability of the other, thus creating an unending spiral of insecurity. According to sober Indian assessments the acquisition of nuclear weapons by Pakistan is not expected in the long run to make a great deal of difference in the advantage that India possesses over Pakistan.

India's advantage is particularly pronounced in the field of nuclear technology and in the development of delivery systems. K. Subrahmanyam former director of institute of defence and strategic analysis (IDSA) has stated that "we need not be unduly perturbed about Pakistan's nuclear capability. Once India decides to build an arsenal it is possible to establish a clear supremacy vis-à-vis Pakistan. With nuclear arsenals on both sides of the border there should be stability of deterrence."[45] In this regard it is worth reiterating that the Indian nuclear-weapons programme and its strategic doctrine are primarily determined not by Pakistan's nuclear potential, but by the existence of Chinese nuclear capabilities. Any political edge that India's nuclear-weapons capacity might be able to give New Delhi over Islamabad would essentially be a bonus. This is so because India's conventional capabilities are sufficient to prevent Pakistan from changing the status quo in the subcontinent in any significant way.

On the nuclear equation there seems to India's supremacy. The report of 1988 sponsored by the Carnegie Endowment for International Peace[46] had concluded that by 1991 Pakistan could have as many as 15 Hiroshima-size bombs, and India could have more than 100.[47] The "missile gap" between India and Pakistan and the greater sophistication of India's technological base makes it clear that in the long duration the only major outcome of the Pakistani quest for nuclear capability would be to give greater legitimacy to an eventual Indian decision to manufacture and deploy nuclear weapons.

India favours preserving the status-quo in Kashmir and Pakistan advocates changing it a situation of nuclear deterrence will make no difference to the Indian decision on this issue. The divergence between India and Pakistan has also been evident in their respective positions on Afghanistan. The policy of Zia-Ul-Haq of putting into power the most fundamentalist and pro-Pakistani factions have made India uneasy as it threatened to change the traditional friendly equation between India and Afghanistan. While basically suspicious of any superpower military intervention in a Third World state, India refused to publicly condemn Moscow for its invasion of Afghanistan.

Indian decision to postpone the SAARC summit scheduled in November 1999 on the pretext of military takeover in Pakistan came as a severe setback to SAARC. The annual SAARC summit was to be hosted by Nepal. India forced Nepal to defer the meeting. The Indian foreign ministry spokesman is reported to have said, "On account of the military coup d'état and consequent concerns and disquiet expressed in the region and beyond, the Government of India has informed the SAARC chairperson in Nepal, the host country of the next SAARC summit, that in the interest of SAARC and of a productive meeting, it would be appropriate to defer the summit for the time-being."[48] This stand of India surprised all the member countries and most of the members were averse to Indian stand. However, they were left with no choice and succumbed to Indian pressure.

Neither, India's call for postponement of the summit owing to the political changes in a member state was supported by the SAARC Charter. The Charter forbids the interference in the internal affairs of the member states. India's objection to military takeover in Pakistan contradicts its past practice of dealing-with martial law regimes of Ayub Khan, Zia-ur-Rahman and Ershad Hussain in Bangladesh. In the SAARC community, Bhutan is ruled by an absolute monarch while Nepal has been moving from dynastic rule to parliamentary democracy. In fact, the idea of SAARC was conceived by military ruler Zia-ur-Rahman and espoused by General Zia-Ul-Haq and the hereditary monarchs of the Himalayan states of Nepal and Bhutan. There is no provision in the Charter of the SAARC or even the United Nations that military rulers are ineligible for membership.[49]

In case of ASEAN one can see that it is a body consisting of states ranging from authoritarian to democratic set up for decades, Indonesia had been ruled by the military ruler General Suharto. Similarly, Brunei, a Sultanate and Burma under military rulers were admitted to the membership of ASEAN. Pakistan denounced India for forcing the postponement of the SAARC summit and accused it of compulsive hostility towards Pakistan. "This represents a gross breach of the established norms of interstate relations, as well as the SAARC charter," a foreign ministry statement maintained. Expressing his concern over the Indian attitude, a Pakistan Foreign Office spokesman termed the postponement of SAARC summit as highly regrettable. He maintained that such interference had been made for the first time and an extreme bad precedent had been set for SAARC. It would also prove highly harmful for the region. He also referred the statement of the present chairman of SAARC which contained several points: firstly, SAARC has no role of interference in political affairs of other countries; secondly, its charter doesn't allow such things; thirdly, the summit meeting was postponed, it will inflict a big blow to the process of cooperation and economic development in the region.

The political role played by India to isolate Pakistan has caused grave concerns among the member countries about the future of SAARC. India was opposed to the political role of SAARC and never agreed to discuss bilateral conflicting issues at that forum. This obviously denies the concept of multilateral cooperation. The Organisation was formed on the principle that all decisions would be taken by the consensus of all the countries, but Indian act to impose its decision on the member countries confirmed the suspicions of all the smaller states against India about its intentions to dominate the region.

India as a Regional Leader: Policies and Perceptions

India can foster regional cooperation given the potential for it and because all the ills of South Asia revolve around the head of India.

Propaganda is made about effective role of India in regional integration but that is far from truth, because its approach towards regional cooperation in South Asia has no takers. India can be held responsible for South Asian regional instability. India has tended to prefer bilateral engagements within the region and avoided multilateral ones to suit its ambitious policies and downplays regional cooperation by focusing on building bilateral alliances. While this stand does not negate the possibility of regional integration, it adversely affects its prospectus. Hence India's policies of avoiding leadership role have led to perceptions of abandonment of its regional responsibilities. South Asia being notorious for lack of cooperation has inherent potential for harmony and cooperation but the need is to explore possibilities in a multilateral set up. South Asian association for regional cooperation (SAARC) needs to provide that platform for resolving both economic and security problems and India needs to strengthen any regional initiative for a better future of South Asia.

It is genuine that India's size and level of development enjoins on it the responsibility of being the natural leader in the process of South Asian development.[50] In dealing with regional concerns India claims to perform its leadership role by pursuing policies to further the common interest of regional states. But the hesitant and cautious policies pursued by India contradict the qualities of dynamic leadership. On the pretext of countering regional apprehensions, India has on many occasions abandoned the leadership mantle. Ironically such policies have fuelled allegations of lack of interest on India's part for regional concerns. Hence India's policies of avoiding leadership have led to perceptions of abandonment of regional responsibilities. Dynamism is the most basic quality of leadership, which has not been demonstrated by India. India has shown reluctance for updating the Indo-Nepal Treaty of 1950 and the Indo-Bangladesh Treaty of 1972 despite repeated demands by the two states. The Indo-Bhutan Treaty of 1949 was updated only recently in 2007.

Diplomatic dynamism implies making the right move when time is opportune; a characteristic missing in India's regional manoeuvres. The insistence by India for signing a five year agreement with Bangladesh allowing it to transport goods to the North-East of India at the sidelines of the SAARC Summit in Sri Lanka in early August 2008 reflects the political naiveté of India. Without getting an assurance from Bangladesh on the issue, a public statement by the India's Ministry of External Affairs on the possibility of signing an agreement only contributed in straining bilateral relations. Moreover expecting the Caretaker Government of Bangladesh to decide on such a sensitive issue demonstrates how distanced is India's approach from the regional realities. In dealing with national political crisis, the South Asian states expect India to play a determining role.

Ibrahim Hussain Zaki of Maldivian Democratic Party expected India to play a more active role in ensuring that true democracy is ushered in Maldives, rather than strengthening the hands of the dictatorial regime through defence packages.[51] Former Nepalese Minister, Keshab Badal told The Hindu, "We urge the Indian Government not to lend support to the Nepal government that could end up with the latter turning even more repressive towards the movement for democracy in Nepal. We seek the sympathy of the Indian Government in our endeavours to replace the monarchy in Nepal with a democratic republic".[52] By officially disassociating herself from such regional pleas India makes a phoney attempt to emerge as a neutral variable in the intra-national and intra-regional politics. The Sri Lankan crisis of the late 1980s has led India to adopt an over-cautious policy with regard to the problems of the Island state. The Indian government has refused to respond the requests for arms supplies, allowing the Sri Lankan government to procure similar supplies from Pakistan and China.

The neighbour's perceptions could be cited as reasons for abandoning leadership on political issues but the regional economic concerns are essentially a victim of India's lack of insight and innovativeness. India remains uninterested in opening its market to the neighbours. Instead of leading the charge towards a rapid reintegration of the South Asian economic space, India remains hesitant in its approach. Security arguments are cited to prevent economic cooperation. India has not evolved a positive approach to deal with the issue of labour migration from Nepal and Bangladesh.

The policy of erecting barbed wires to deal with labour migration negates the leadership potential of India in the region. India continues to ignore the regional realities by emphasising on duty free trade, while the real constraints to intra-regional trade are to be found in tariff and para-tariff barriers. Gujral Doctrine best illustrates this reality. It is important to note that the Gujral Doctrine is not an innovative Indian policy to allay fears of neighbours. It is a standard practice in international relations for the bigger states to grant concessions to the smaller countries. J.N. Dixit while voicing this concern has stated that such gestures of generosity (Gujral Doctrine) 'smacks of a certain incipient big brotherly hegemonistic attitude'.[53]

India has not genuinely applied the Doctrine on ground. For example, trade concessions to Bangladesh for a long time were made contingent on their giving transit rights. The discrepancy between India's rhetoric and action is evident from the example below. India's External Affairs Minister Yashwant Sinha had stated that India is seeking to institutionalise positive asymmetry in favour of our neighbour's.[54]

India has put forth proposals for the free movement of media persons and media products in South Asia and the establishment of cultural sub-centres under the main SAARC Cultural Centre in Kandy. At the Fourteenth SAARC Summit held in 2007, India offered unilateral concessions in the form of allowing duty free access to goods from the least developed countries of South Asia. India also initiated discussions on establishing a South Asia University and working towards creating a common currency for the region. India tends to support or endorse rather than initiate and facilitate new regional ventures; India rarely champions the group interest at the international forums; rather than promoting group behaviour and diluting group differences within SAARC, India tends to disassociate[55] issues and manage them at the bilateral level, regional goal setting and formulation of collective strategies are not explicitly pursued by India. India's regional policies do not exhibit the ability to make short-term concessions for securing long-term goals. In the face of negative perceptions India is exercising the option of restrained leadership, which needs to be replaced by a more pro-active leadership role for countering the adverse perceptual mould in the region.

Notes

1. Lange Knapp and et al., (2012), "Revisiting Contemporary South Asia: Politics, Economics and Security", *Institute for Transnational Studies*, Italy, pp. 158-159.
2. *Ibid.*
3. Annual Report (2003-04), *Indian Ministry of External Affairs,* p. 1.
4. Raja Mohan C. (2004), *Crossing The Rubicon*, New York; Palgrave Macmillan, p. 262.
5. Lange Knapp and et al., (2012), "Revisiting Contemporary South Asia: Politics, Economics and Security", *Institute for Transnational Studies*, Italy, pp. 158-159.
6. *Ibid.*
7. Wilson D. and P. Roopa (2003), "Dreaming with the BRICs: The path to 2050", *Goldman Sachs Global Economics paper*, No. 99, p. 4.
8. Lange, Knapp and et al., (2012), "Revisiting Contemporary South Asia: Politics, Economics and Security", *Institute for Transnational Studies*, Italy, p. 160.
9. Akram, A.I. (1985), "Security of Small States: Implications for South Asia", *Regional Studies*, Vol. 3, No. 3, Islamabad, p. 8.
10. Bhasin, Madhav (2008), "India's Role in South Asia – Perceived Hegemony or Reluctant Leadership, *Indian Foreign Affairs*, *globalindiafoundation,* Vol. 3, no. 4, p.7.
11. Jayewardene, Junius Richard, President of Sri Lanka, at the Fourth SAARC Summit, Concluding Session, 29-3, Dec. 1988, Islamabad, Pakistan, *From SARC to SAARC: Milestones in the Evolution of Regional Cooperation in South Asia (1980-88*) Vol. I, SAARC Secretariat, Kathmandu.
12. Jain, B.M. (1987), *South Asia, India, and United States*, RBSA Publishers, Jaipur, p 25.
13. Ayoob Mohammad. (1991), "India as a Regional Hegemon: External Opportunities and Internal Constraints", *International Journal.* Vol. 46. No. 31, p. 420.
14. Chopra, Pran (1993), "*The Crisis of Foreign Policy: Perspective and Issues,*" Wheeler Publications, Allahabad, pp. 45-46.
15. Harshe Rajeri and Sethi K.M.(2005), "*Critical Reflections on India's Foreign Policy"*, Orient Longman, New Delhi, p. 210.
16. Bahadur, Kalim and Lama, P Mahindra (1995), "*New Perspectives on India Nepal Relations"*, Har Anand, New Delhi, pp.140-141.
17. Rizvi, Gowher (1993), *"South Asia in a Changing International Order",* Sage publications, New Delhi, pp. 34-35.
18. Harshe, Rajeri and Sethi, K.M.(2005), "*Critical Reflections on India's Foreign Policy"*, Orient Longman, New Delhi, p. 212.

19. Upreti, B.C. (1996), *"The Nepali immigrants in Bhutan: Growing Conflict between National and Ethnic Identities", Indus Publishers,* New Delhi, pp. 78-79.
20. Harshe, Rajeri and Sethi K.M.(2005), *"Critical Reflections on India's Foreign Policy"*, Orient Longman, New Delhi, p. 212.
21. *Ibid.*
22. *Ibid.*
23. The Guardian National daily Newspaper published in Britain.
24. Bhasin, Madhav (2008), "India's Role in South Asia – Perceived Hegemony or Reluctant Leadership, *Indian Foreign Affairs, globalindiafoundation*, Vol. 3, No. 4, p. 11.
25. *Ibid.*
26. N.S. Sisodia and C. Uday Bhaskar (2005), "*Emerging India-Security and Foreign Policy Perspectives"*, IDSA and Promilla & Co. Publishers, New Delhi, p. 299.
27. Bhasin, Madhav (2008), "India's Role in South Asia – Perceived Hegemony or Reluctant Leadership, *Indian Foreign Affairs, globalindiafoundation*, Vol. 3, No. 4, p. 12.
28. Sagan, D. Scott (2001) , "The Perils of Proliferation in South Asia," *Asian Survey,* Vol. 41, No. 6 , California, pp. 1064-1086.
29. Hagerty, Devin. T.(1991), "India's Regional Security Doctrine," *Asian Survey,* Vol. 31, No. 4. California, p. 360.
30. Bhasin, Madhav (2008), "India's Role in South Asia – Perceived Hegemony or Reluctant Leadership", *Indian Foreign Affairs, globalindiafoundation*, Vol. 3, No. 4, p. 13.
31. Dixit, J. N., "Awaiting Indian Initiative", *Indian Express*, January 2, 1996.
32. Bjorn Hettne & et al. (1998), *"National Perspectives on the New Regionalism in the South Asia*", Vol.3, Macmillan, London, pp. 127-128.
33. *SAARC Survey of Development and Cooperation, 1998-1999,* Research and Information System for Developing Countries, New Delhi, pp. 82-83.
34. Bhasin, Madhav (2008), "India's Role in South Asia – Perceived Hegemony or Reluctant Leadership", *Indian Foreign Affairs, globalindiafoundation*, Vol. 3, no. 4, p. 15.
35. Shome, Parthasarthy (2001), *"India and Economic Cooperation in South Asia"*, Indian Council for Research on International Economic Relations, p. 38.
36. Jetly, Nancy and Gonsalves, Eric (1999), *"Dynamics of South Asia Regional Cooperation and SAARC"*, Sage Publications, New Delhi, p. 95.
37. Government of India, Annual Report, 1999-2000, *Ministry of External Affairs*, p. 2.

38. Mohan, C. Raja (2007), "*India's New Regionalism*", Himaal, Nepal, pp. 5-6.
39. Taneja, Nisha (2005), Informal trade in South Asia? How to channelize to a formal route? CUTS briefing paper RECSA.
40. Nihal, Pitigala (2005), What Does Regional Trade in South Asia Reveal about Future Trade Integration? Some Empirical Evidence World Bank Policy Research Working Paper, 3497.
41. H.L.D. Mahindapala (2007), "India must apologize to SAARC for exporting terrorism and destabilizing the region," *Asian Tribune*, World Institute for Asian Studies, Vol. 11, No. 563.
42. *Ibid.*
43. Ayoob, Mohammed (1989-90), "India in South Asia: The Quest for Regional Predominance", *World Policy Journal*, Vol. 7, No. 1, winter, New York, p. 115.
44. Askari, Rizvi Hasan (1989), "The legacy of military rule in Pakistan" *survival*, global politics and strategy, Vol. 31, No. 3, p. 267.
45. Ayoob, Mohammad (1976), "India and Pakistan: Prospects for Detente" *Pacific Community*, Vol. 8, No. 1, pp. 149-169.
46. Rasul, B Rais (1985), "Pakistan's Nuclear Program: Prospects for Proliferation," *Asian Survey*, California Vol. 25, No. 4, p. 472.
47. This is a private nonprofit organisation dedicated to advancing cooperation among nations and it's headquarter is in Washington. D.C.
48. Carnegie Task Force on Non-Proliferation and South Asian Security, Nuclear Weapons and South Asian Security (Washington, DC: Carnegie Endowment for International Peace, 1988), p. 56.
49. Taneja, Nisha (2005), *Informal trade in South Asia? How to channelise to a formal route*? CUTS briefing paper RECSA 5/2005.
50. Pitigala Nihal (2005), *What Does Regional Trade in South Asia Reveal about Future Trade Integration*? Some Empirical Evidence World Bank Policy Research Working Paper, 3497.
51. Bhasin, Madhav (2008), "India's Role in South Asia – Perceived Hegemony or Reluctant Leadership, *Indian Foreign Affairs, globalindiafoundation*. Vol. 3, No. 4, p. 16.
52. *Ibid.*
53. *Ibid.*
54. Sharma, R.R. (2006), India and Emerging Asia, Sage Publications, New Delhi, pp. 77-78.

Chapter - 4

India and SAARC: Challenges and Opportunities

South Asia is seen as a geo-strategic, geo-economic unit by some and a single civilisation by others. The programme of regional cooperation was expected to benefit immensely from the historical and cultural ties connecting people across national borders in South Asia. Such assessments created positive possibilities regarding cooperation in the region. SAARC was expected to be an instrument for the "promotion of peace, progress and stability in this part of the world." It was also to enhance sovereignty and foster peace, freedom and social justice among member states. It was supposed to be a framework for the promotion of the welfare and prosperity of the peoples and the improvement of their quality of life". The dilemmas and contradictions inherent in South Asian Cooperation have resulted from the simultaneous impact of different forces.

Regionalism has a different meaning and purpose for each nation when they become a part of any regional organisation.[1] In most cases, states that join hands in any regional cooperation mechanism have certain basic differences; for most regional cooperation is limited only to economic cooperation through free-trade agreements. Differences among member states of the regional organisations are greater in the presence of inter-state conflict(s) between the member states. Even if states seem to agree on some issues at the platform of that particular regional cooperation organisation, their intentions behind the concept and purpose of regionalism are fundamentally different. Inter-state conflicts have been the most daunting challenges of the process of regionalism. This phenomenon is clearly visible in the functioning of the SAARC.[2]

Established with a vision to forge a South Asian identity, SAARC has been unable to fulfill this promise and has often been criticised for its failures and shortcomings. Some constraining factors that can be identified in the SAARC framework are: its inability to tackle inter-state conflicts that has often made it hostage to bilateral conflicts and the nationalistic interests of member states. Apart from this, an Indo-centric strategic perception exists both among India's neighbours as well as among the big players in global relationship. SAARC was born with different disabilities and constraints, which were essentially self-imposed. It adopted a functional approach of cooperation in non-controversial areas like social and cultural fields, hoping that if successfully carried forward, opportunities for cooperation in more vital areas could open up. Moreover, SAARC follows the principles that all decisions have to be made unanimously and that no bilateral and contentious issue can be made on the SAARC agenda. This clearly exhibits a weaker inter-state relationship toward equitable participation in policy-making for South Asian people.[3]

Although cooperation among SAARC countries was supposed to be based on areas of mutual cooperation, with the exclusion of bilateral and contentious issues, it is the latter that has derailed the success of SAARC. Since the partition of British India into the Republic of India and the Islamic Republic of Pakistan in 1947, the Kashmir issue has been one of the main obstacles preventing the SAARC region from achieving its full economic potential as a regional grouping.[4] For example, the postponement of the SAARC Heads of State Summit in 1999 followed renewed tensions between India and Pakistan. Similarly, both countries' preferential imports declined significantly from 1996 to 1998 following the nuclear tests in 1998 and the Kargil conflict in 1999.[5] The way forward for SAARC to achieve greater regional economic cooperation will mean dealing with bilateral and contentious issues such as the Kashmir dispute. In this context, political will and a change of mindset is crucial to resolve economic obstacles like the Kashmir dispute if the SAARC region does not wish to fall further economically.

India and SAARC

In South Asia, India accounts for 72 per cent of the total area, 77 per cent of the population and 78 per cent of the regional Gross National Product.[6] The geographical uniqueness and its rapid economic growth makes India stand out as a logical driver for the success of the SAARC.[7] The enabling and constraining capabilities of India with regard to promoting regional cooperation in South Asia had been discussed even before the conceptual journey of the SAARC began in 1983. India occupies a unique position in the South Asian region. By the virtue of its size, location and economic potential, India assumes a natural leadership role in the region, but the overbearing presence of a neighbour with aspirations for global leadership has also been a source of apprehensions for the other South Asian countries. India claims a leadership position for herself, while her South Asian neighbours accuse of her emerging hegemony.[8]

Table 4.1: Some Basic Economic indicators of SAARC Countries

Country	*Population (2011)*	*Area (Sq. Kms.)*	*GDP in US $ (Purchasing Power Parity -2010)*	*GDP Growth Rate (2010)*
Afghanistan	29.8 million	652,230	$ 29.81 billion	8.9 %
Bangladesh	158.6 million	143,998	$ 259.30 billion	6.0 %
Bhutan	0.7 Million	38,394	$ 03.50 billion	6.8 %
India	1.2 billion	3,287,263	$ 04.04 trillion	8.3 %
Maldives	0.4 Million	298	$ 01.80 billion	4.0 %
Nepal	29.4 million	147,351	$ 35.31 billion	3.5 %
Pakistan	187.3 million	796,095	$ 451.20 billion	2.7%
Sri Lanka	21.3 million	65610	$ 104.7 billion	6.9%

Selected Development Indicators of SAARC Members.[9]

India is also a constant factor in most of the inter-state disputes within the region; some owe their origin to the colonial past.[10] India has a range of issues with Bangladesh, Nepal and Sri Lanka including sharing of waters and borders, illegal migration, trade and transit relations and perceptions of inappropriate Indian interference in the internal affairs of others.[11] There are other inter-state conflicts too which do not involve India, but these are less significant compared to those involving India.[12] The strained relations between India-Pakistan are the most severe obstacle to regional cooperation within the framework of SAARC.[13] The Kashmir issue and Pakistan's support for cross-border terrorism continues to underscore the brittle relationship between India and Pakistan which seriously impedes the SAARC growth.[14] Pakistan has consistent involvement in undermining India's leadership role in the region.[15] While addressing the sixteenth SAARC Summit, Maldivian President Mohamed Nasheed in a direct reference, blamed India and Pakistan for making the SAARC non-functional.[16] Similarly, Jigme Thinley, Bhutan's Prime Minister, in his opening address at the same Summit stated that, 'fractious and quarrelsome neighbours do not make a prosperous community'.[17] India considers that the SAARC provides an opportunity to the smaller nations to collectively oppose its interests.[18] Some nations of the region have forged ties with China to balance the influence of India.[19] Nepal, Bangladesh and Pakistan's initiative in campaigning for China's entry into the SAARC as an observer is viewed by India as an attempt to marginalise its influence in the region.[20] The indifferent attitude of the smaller nations towards India besides dampening the spirit of SAARC vitiates the environment for India and makes it reluctant to take on leadership within the region.[21] Suspicion and mistrust amongst the member states, 'serve as a stumbling block in the way of moving towards substantive areas of cooperation within the framework of SAARC'.[22]

More Theoretical than Practical

The single most important weakness of the SAARC process has not been in the domain of ideas but their execution. Although there is no dearth of bright ideas but most of them are not pursued to their logical end. This is true for both governmental and non-governmental sectors. In the official SAARC process non-implementation of decisions can be identified at three different levels:

(i) The Technical Committees do not follow-up the decisions, resulting in their repetitive reiteration year after year;

(ii) The findings and recommendations of workshops and seminars generally remain on paper;

(iii) The decisions taken by the First Special Session of the Standing Committee and even the plans and projects specifically recommended by various specific ministerial groups are not seriously implemented.[23]

Terrorism in South Asia

In South Asia, terrorism has been a factor influencing interstate relations for a long time now. India and Pakistan have a conflictual relation on the issue of terrorism. India accuses Pakistan and its ISI (Inter Service Intelligence) of sponsoring cross-border terrorism in Jammu and Kashmir and North East and encouraging internal violence all over India. While Pakistan blames India of inciting ethnic and separatist strife in Pakistan. The relations between the two worsened further after terrorist attack on the Indian Parliament in December 2001, which saw India threatening to launch a full-scale war to end the cross-border terrorism.[24] This situation proved detrimental for the weakening of regional security. India also had complaints against Myanmar, Bhutan, Nepal and Bangladesh for allowing the terrorist organsations of North eastern India to utilise their territories to run terrorist camps. Sri Lanka, on the other hand, had problems with India as Sri Lankan government accuses India of helping Tamil terrorists operating in Sri Lanka. Examples of cooperation are limited but worth mentioning. There has been cooperation between India and Nepal in 1950's to deal with political revolts in Nepal and India sent its troops to pressurise the (Liberation Tigers of Tamil Eelam) LTTE for the implementation of 1987 agreement. On regional level, the third SAARC summit in Kathmandu (1987) adopted a resolution to suppress terrorism, which was further reinforced in the Summit of 2001. After September 11, 2001 attack on Pentagon and World Trade Center (WTC) in America there has been a renewed effort by the US to cooperate with the South Asian countries to end the South Asian nexus of global terrorism.

Western Outlook

Though the SAARC has granted observer status to the European Union and eight other countries[25], the West still looks at South Asia as two entities: 'Western South Asia', comprising Afghanistan,

Pakistan and India and 'Eastern South Asia' which includes the other countries.[26] The West attaches significant importance to the former due to the US-led involvement in the 'Global War on Terrorism' (GWOT) and its relationship with India, considered a rising power. On the other hand 'Eastern South Asia', is considered as a less significant region for the West, as it offers very little of economic or strategic interest. After the defeat of the LTTE in Sri Lanka and the process of Maoist soldiers being re-integrated into Nepalese society, there are no major political issues of concern to the West.[27] The SAARC, therefore, does not enjoy the same level of Western support as ASEAN and other regional organisations did. Finally, while SAARC has yet to devise a conflict management norm – informal or otherwise – the presence of extra-regional powers in the organisation and region appears to have reduced the chances of armed inter-state conflict in South Asia. Much of this also has to do with the rapprochement between India, the largest member of the regional organisation, and the US. Traditionally, India has regarded the superpower with suspicion, given its close alliance with Pakistan.[28] However, in the early Twenty-first century some factors have brought the U.S. and India closer together. Apart from India's growing economic openness, a mutual suspicion of China's rise and an interest in countering terrorism have changed Indian perceptions of the US and the latter is increasingly seen as a fair arbiter.[29]

SAARC and Environmental Issues

Climate change is one of the most serious challenges faced by humanity in our times. This challenge is more serious for the developing world especially the South Asia. The poorest are the most vulnerable to the effects of climate change, having the least resource from the status quo and minimum protection from the environmental shifts. The World Bank in its approach paper observes that in South Asia around 600 million people subsist on less than US $1.25 a day. Hence even a small variation in climatic conditions can cause irreversible losses and dip large numbers into destitution. The vestiges of effect of climate change can be seen in a simple estimate: over 50 per cent of the South Asians, i.e., more than 750 million people- have been affected by natural disasters in the last decades. The human and economic toll has been high with almost 230,000 deaths and about US $ 45 billion in damages.[30]

Climate change has also social and political consequences.[31] To a great extent it might increase the volatility of weak or failing states by overstretching the already limited capacity of governments to respond effectively to challenges that they face. It could even destabilise well-off and emerging countries and even the entire regions because of the inability of the governments to provide protection in the face of climate change. It could aggravate hardship and trigger frustration leading to tensions between different ethnic and religious groups within and between countries. Climate change will alter rainfall patterns and further reduce available fresh water by as much as 20-30 per cent in certain regions.

Since its inception SAARC has taken significant initiatives on environmental issues and combating climate. The third SAARC summit which was convened in Kathmandu, Nepal on November 2-4, 1987, decided to commission a study on the protection and preservation of the environment and the causes and consequences of natural disasters' in a well-planned comprehensive framework. In fact, while deciding to constitute a commission in this study, the summit leaders expressed their deep concern at the rapid and continuing degradation of the environment including extensive destruction of forests in the South Asian region. They also noted that South Asia was afflicted with such natural disasters as floods, droughts, cyclones, tidal waves which have had a particularly severe impact causing immense human suffering. This study which was finalised in December 1991 was formulated after very comprehensive national studies by individual member states to bring out the conditions prevalent in the countries of the region on environment and natural disasters. The individual country reports also mentioned the preventive and remedial measures taken with regard to adverse climatic conditions and natural disasters. The individual country studies were amalgamated with the help of consultant experts. The report noted that the region is one of the poorest in the world and has a high rate of population growth and population density and further the SAARC member states comprise 20 per cent of the world's population living on 3.5 per cent of the total land area and generate only 2 per cent of the world's GNP.[32]

SAARC environment ministers meeting in Dhaka in 2008 adopted SAARC Action Plan on climate change. The objectives of the action plan were to identify and create opportunities for activities achievable through regional cooperation and South–South support in terms of technology and knowledge transfer, to provide impetus for regional level activities and to support the global negotiation process of UNFCCC[33] such as Bali action plan, through a common understanding or elaboration of the various negotiating issues to effectively reflect the concerns of SAARC member states.[34]

Democratic Crisis

The political culture prevalent in South Asia has not seen much of a democracy. Many of them have had their shares of problems with military coups, despotic monarchies and other non-democratic features. And India often had to bear the brunt of undemocratic policies executed by some of its neighbours. This has affected bilateral relations in some form and SAARC has been the loser in the final count. A form of 'democratic and other socio-economic culture exchange' is always welcome among the SAARC nations.[35] Differences in political systems also make regional cooperation difficult. Except for India, none of SAARC's members have a stable, secular democracy. Unfortunately, the convergence of political systems is unlikely in the near future. The problem was aggravated in the past because of India's pro-democracy rhetoric. In recent times, however, this problem has to some extent changed because on the one hand India has toned down its rhetoric, and on the other hand democracy has begun to put down roots in SAARC countries such as Bangladesh, Bhutan, Maldives and Nepal, while Sri Lanka is actively encouraging its Tamil minorities to participate in the democratic process.[36]

Dynamics of Intra and Inter-State Conflicts in South Asia

There is no single particular factor/reason as the main cause of conflict in South Asia. It is embroiled in many issues and provides a disappointing picture in every social, economic and political context. This is due to the fact that South Asia is almost perpetually plagued by various inter and intra-state conflicts and crisis stemming from the lackadaisical approach of the ruling elite towards resolution of such problems which are based on narrow considerations of caste, religion, ethnicity, language, community and after different selected problems. This distorts the national integrity/unity and the overall order and situation of the affected states. In other words, the persistence of multifarious problems, both within and between the South Asian states hampers the sustenance of an environment wherein basic essential needs of the common man are fulfilled.[37] Furthermore, South Asia is an area of tremendous political complexities. States like Pakistan and Bangladesh have been largely ruled by authoritarian military rulers. India per se faces several unresolved issues that stem from internal as well as external sources. These include ethnicity, border disputes, separatist demands, terrorism and subversive activities, communalism, religious problems and so on. All these issues flout the basic ideals of nation building in India, that is, the ideals of democracy, secularism, socialism and federalism. The political fundamentalists such as Maoists and mainstream political parties are posing major threat to democracy in Nepal.[38] In addition to creating law and order problems, increased human rights violations and a heavy reliance on security forces have undermined the question of legitimacy of governance in Nepal. Moreover, the problem of civil violence in recent years has emerged as a more serious security issue than the problem of inter-state warfare in South Asia. India has been variously preoccupied with quelling separatists and religious conflicts such as in the state of Punjab and Kashmir (an issue that remains contentious between India and Pakistan), for the separatists, Mizoram, Assam, and Nagaland (Eastern India) for an autonomy and in Gujarat, Mumbai and other parts have certain religious, ethnic, psychological and economic underpinnings. Sri Lanka has also had its own set of problems. Democracy in this tiny island nation remains overshadowed by the civil war emanating from Tamil-Sinhalese ethnic conflicts. These conflicts in Sri Lanka have pushed successive governments on the brink of collapse. Ruling elites in Sri Lanka failed to reform economic policies due to polarised political debate.[39] In Pakistan, the society faces sporadic bursts of violence derived from ethnic, sectarian and religious differences. For instance, conflict in the Sindh province between ethnic Sindhis and those residents who migrated from India following partition has made the province ungovernable. Conservative religious elements are also very powerful in Pakistan leading to tensions and conflicts over religious differences, which has also played a major role in sustaining the Indo-Pakistan altercations over Kashmir.[40] The emerging internal political problems in Bhutan and the fallout of attempted coup in Maldives in 1987 have varying affects in uniting the country for the cause of development. All this can largely be attributed to the fact that political and governing institutions in most of the South Asian countries are weak while the political parties themselves lack vigour, organisation, discipline and commitments. Taken individually, each of the South Asian states suffer from some kind of instability and consequently projects varying intensities of human deprivation.

Inter-State Conflicts

South Asia is one of the critical regions with complex security in the world primarily due to the fact that most of the South Asian states are engulfed with varying degrees of conflicts and disputes. Inter-state conflicts in South Asia probably are highest compared to any other regional blocs. Bilateral relations are defined by antagonism and mistrust. The differences between India and Pakistan over Kashmir, between Sri Lanka and India over the nationality of Tamilians where Sri Lanka accused India especially the state government of Tamil Nadu for supplying arms and providing trainings to the Tamil terrorists in its Southern areas are only two of the most outstanding examples in this regard.[41] The dispute between India and Bangladesh over illegal migration from the Chittagong Hill Tracts (CHT), demarcation of boundaries involving fertile islands and enclaves and also in sharing the water of river Ganges.[42]

The retreat of the British Raj and the ensuing bitterness generated between the ruling elites of the two major South Asian states gravely disrupted the traditional complementarities and cohesion. Indeed, the legacy of state formation in South Asia bestows a unique complexity to the entire region. Thus, some of the contentious issues that inhibit cooperation in South Asia include those resulting from colonial legacies, issues of political and ideological character, issues of strategic conflict and military balance, issues that arise from the spill-over effect of internal conflicts and turmoil in a given country on its neighbours and issues that arise out of resource and developmental conflicts.

The most pronounced security dilemma stems from escalating arms race in South Asia, particularly between the two military powers India and Pakistan. These disputes among countries further complicate the scenario and have created a lot of problems among the leaders for friendly talks. This situation deficits confidence building measures (CBMs). They are meant to address precisely this kind of situation in the region and obstruct any sort of operationalisation of Free Trade Area or much talked South Asian Free Trade Area (SAFTA). Similarly the cultural diversity based on languages, religions and ethnicities is another factor that disabled region to unite. Rather it frequently exerts a negative impact on inter-state relations in South Asia due to religious differences. For example, Pakistan's deep commitment to create an Islamic state and Bharatia Janata Party's (BJP's) commitment to make India purely a Hindu state are two kind of school of thoughts that hampers nation making in South Asia.

The area is characterised by countries with widely differing political systems–democracies, military dictatorships and monarchies. Though most of the South Asian states have emerged with shared colonial pasts, similar political experiences, common social values divergences, however, are still significant. India and Sri Lanka have performed better than other functioning democracies with varying degrees of success. Pakistan and Bangladesh, at the beginning of the 1990s witnessed a sweeping democratic transition in their domestic scenarios. Nepal's transition to democracy is at the crossroad following the Maoist movement.[43]

The Indian political system has been professedly a blend of democracy, federalism, secularism and until its global collapse socialism. Bangladesh and Pakistan are Islamic states where the influence of religion runs very high as an instrument of political profiteering rather than indicator of prevailing public opinion. Maldives is an Islamic society with relatively lesser influence of religion in politics. Nepal remains under Hindu influence while Bhutan and Sri Lanka are Buddhists societies. South Asia presents as different political order and powers structures as one seldom finds in any other geo-political region of the world.[44] South Asian nations despite their apparent adherence to the ideal of nonalignment have pursued extremely disconsonant foreign policies. Consequently, the major global powers have played their roles in aggravating the intra-regional cleavages of South Asia. Finally, India's overwhelming regional preponderance creates certain basic insecurities and sharp differences between India and its neighbourhood. All these aspects have created a multitude of problems for the South Asian region. These problems collectively boil down to a crisis of legitimacy, welfare and order in the affected area.

The troubles in South Asia, its endemic tensions, mutual distrust and occasional hostilities are largely considered products of the contradictions of India's security perception vis-à-vis that of the rest of the countries of the area. India's neighbours perceive threats to their security coming primarily from India whereas India considers neighbours as an integral part of its own security system. There has always been certain psychological misgiving on the part of the smaller states about their all-powerful neighbour India. This has also been the main cause of failure of the SAARC to evolve as true regional bloc.

Since its inception in 1983 there have also been serious differences among member countries over the aims and functioning of SAARC.[45] Such differences have been pronounced in verbal bickering in several SAARC meetings. This is in the face of the fact that closer social, economic and cultural ties (the espoused ideals of SAARC) are considered the only hope for building regional cooperation efforts in South Asia in the coming years. Indeed, increasing rationalisation of world trade and the fluidity of the emerging global system has increased trade within each trade blocs and those countries that do not belong to any trade blocs are likely to be the losers.[46] This also provides a strong rationale for sustaining the SAARC vis-à-vis future trade prospects of South Asia. The failure of SAARC arises precisely out of the effort to use the institution to focus attention away from serious disagreements within the member countries and establish some arrangements despite these disagreements.[47] India, which is a key player in the region has continuously followed a repressive and suppressive policy in the name of cooperation and has flexed its military might on the relatively smaller countries in the region.[48] Unless an institution comes to possess the ability to harness (or at least moderate) such play, it can only play a marginal role in promoting regional growth.[49] The assumption that peace can be achieved through SAARC without addressing the political problems of the region has neither been able to cultivate peace nor to invigorate the SAARC process successfully. Though since its very inception it has been regularly able to hold Summit meetings but there are interruptions in between owing mainly to intra-state conflicts between the member countries.[50]

Integration of South Asian Nations

The formation of SAARC is a landmark step taken by the leaders of the region. The main rational behind was to develop a congenial environment through summit diplomacy where all nations could interact peacefully with each other, cultivate sustainable peace and promote mutual economic well being by harnessing available resources in the region through the process of political and economic integration. Nevertheless, after 26 years of establishment, neither South Asian nations have been able to push the process of integration into full swing nor the organisation itself has become viable enough that could promote peace and harmony or prevent conflicts in the region. Paradoxically, South Asia has came into the international limelight in the recent years.

Former American President Bill Clinton described "South Asia as the most dangerous place on earth[51] on the eve of two emerging antagonistic nuclear powers." This has been accompanied by a vigorously renewed interest in studies pertaining to patterns of cooperation and conflict among the major South Asian countries. The main contention here is that South Asia is still in the process of evolving as a 'region' due to two basic factors. Adequate degree of complementarity of interests has not yet been achieved among the South Asian states and the almost perpetual preoccupation with intra-state conflict and crises leaves individual states with scarce time or resources to work towards regional solutions.[52] Therefore, it would be useful to elaborate upon these two points and outline the broad parameters of this study. Basically, a region can be defined on the basis of certain specific indicators that confirm its existence. A set of countries in close geographical proximity with each other can be categorised as a 'region' when, first and foremost, they share a certain commonality of (national) interests. These interests could incorporate a whole gamut of social, economic, political, cultural, historical and other factor's, secondly, this set of countries should be sufficiently enlightened so as to understand the significance of placing cooperation above conflict in the conduct of inter-state relations. This should also be bolstered by a collective desire to come together on a common plank to create some lasting mechanism for regional cooperation.[53] What makes this argument such a significant is that these factors bind people together through social and cultural exchanges due to shared commonality, which ultimately helps countries to extend the same spirit at the state level. But above mentioned sentiments are more or less lacking among the South Asian states. Such a lack of 'region-ness' in South Asia can also be understood in terms of another related phenomenon, that is, the persistence of myriad of social, economic and political problems practically in each and every South Asian state. Therefore such intra-state problems are often either the cause or consequence of inter-state disputes and misperceptions as well. Thus, there emerges an inextricable connection between the internal and external relations of South Asian states with patterns that are further complicated by what has been succinctly explained as the pursuit of order, welfare and legitimacy.[54]

The pace of integration among the South Asian nations has not been satisfactory since the formation of the SAARC. Political and religious tensions run all time high in the region.[55] The World Bank's South Asia regional unit has commenced a study on the subject and identified four conditions that significantly bring success in integrating a region particularly to become FTAs (free trade areas) among a group of nations. First, the World Bank identifies that the pre-FTA tariffs should be high, second, the members of the FTA should be important trading partners before entering into an arrangement. Third, there should be complementarity in demand. Fourth, the difference in economic structure should be based on the 'true' competitiveness of the countries involved.

This means that arrangements with countries that have substantially different factor endowments are superior to those with similar endowments. South Asia hardly satisfies any of the above conditions except the first, in the case of forming a possible South Asian Free Trade Area. South Asian countries trade little with each other but trade much with other nations of the world including, particularly with North America, Europe and Group of Eight (G8) countries.[56] The G8 includes much of NA (North America) and Europe. The composition of each country exports to these regions is almost similar, with the overwhelming share accounted for by ready-made garments. The trade between South Asian countries is more competitive than complementary. India's trade (import plus export) with NAFTA and the EU comprises more than 42 per cent of the total in 1994 and by contrast with the countries of the South Asian region is not more than 10 per cent of the total.[57] Under these circumstances, it is unlikely to maximise gain out of South Asian PTAs (preferential trade areas).

India factor

South Asia as India's exclusive sphere of Influence

South Asia is India's exclusive sphere of influence. There can be very little doubt about the fact that India desires that all the six neighbouring states of South Asia should let her determine the policies and goals of the region. India would also like them to turn for help in solving their problems and meeting the needs for technology. The movement of Indian forces into Sri Lanka in 1987 with reference to the Tamil problem is an illustration of the role India hopes to play in the region.[58] When a small neighbour cannot handle its domestic problems, Delhi will be happy to do so for them, if necessary, by the use of the great military machine which India is building.

It is a common phenomenon in international relations that a small neighbour had to live under fear when its large neighbour has 'expansionist' policy and there are unresolved and complicating factors in their relations. This is particularly true in the case of South Asia as India continuously shows her hegemonic flavour towards her small neighbours rather than being regarded as 'Big Brother'. Bhutan and Nepal are continuously living under this threat of becoming next Sikkim[59] and bilateral disputes are especially acute with each and every country. To some extent India also sees SAARC as a forum for ganging up to withstand Indian hegemonic pressures, which is just an illusion.

To create a sense of 'easiness' among her neighbours, the former Indian Prime Minister I K Gujral adopted a doctrine called 'Gujral Doctrine'[60] as a tool of conflict management in the region. The Gujral Doctrine is a set of five principles to guide the conduct of foreign relations with India's immediate neighbours as spelt out by I.K. Gujral, first as India's foreign minister and later as the Prime Minister. Among other factors, these five principles arise from the belief that India's stature and strength cannot be divorced from the quality of its relations with its neighbours. It recognises the supreme importance of friendly, cordial relations with neighbours. These principles are: first, with neighbours like Bangladesh, Bhutan, Maldives, Nepal and Sri Lanka, India does not ask for reciprocity, but accommodates what it can in good faith and trust; second, no South Asian country should allow its territory to be used against the interest of another country of the region; third, no country should interfere in the internal affairs of another; fourth, all South Asian countries must respect each other's territorial integrity and sovereignty; and, finally, they should settle all their disputes through peaceful bilateral negotiations.[61] But in reality it has never been applied or discussed at the policy level. Indian bureaucrats were sceptical about the idea. Also once Gujral was out of power, the doctrine went with him.

The growing political strife and bureaucratic obstacles indicates that 'non-tariff barriers in the form of political disputes, bureaucratic delays and interference by the intelligence agencies have been obstructing trade between India and Pakistan. There are growing concern that regionalism in South Asia might end up as Pandora's box if concerned efforts are not made beyond the turmoil of political exigencies. Even the newly formed SAPTA has met with extremely limited success in promoting intra-SAARC trade.[62] Similarly, hopes of forming a South Asian Free Trade Area (SAFTA) considered being more unrealistic. For instance, a free trade implies dismantling customs barriers, which means all SAARC members will have to agree on a common import policy, either formally or informally and no country will retain sovereignty over the import policy. However, it is felt that unless countries of a region enjoy considerable political harmony, they cannot possibly agree on concessions like surrendering sovereignty over their import policy. This is particularly true in South Asia where, being the strongest–that is, the Indian economy–will tend to be dominant overall regional outcomes.[63] So, although economic cooperation and even integration is very desirable in South Asia, it calls for creating a politically harmonious subcontinent, which is an extremely formidable task. It implies settling issues like the Kashmir, sharing of land and boundaries with Bangladesh, renegotiating the 1950 Treaty with Nepal and so on. India clearly has the ability to build nuclear weapons and is equally clearly opposed to any other South Asian power acquiring that capacity. In a world which has shown no serious inclinations towards disarmament, the threat of a Nuclear attack on the South Asian region is therefore either going to be met with the help of one of the superpowers or India.[64]

South Asian Economic Cooperation: Prospects

The question that experience of SAPTA (South Asian Preferential Trade Area) negotiations raise is whether South Asian countries are genuinely committed to regional trade liberalisation or whether it is merely a confidence building exercise that is being pursued as a means of easing political tensions in the region. Some take the argument further to insist that economic cooperation will inevitably lead to greater political cohesion in the region and therefore should be pursued even if initial trade related benefits of SAPTA prove very limited. Is this argument valid for South Asia? Are South Asian interests best served by pursuing economic cooperation? Or are the political obstacles too deeply ingrained to justify the costs of negotiating, administering and implementing a regional trade arrangement?

Some political economists have drawn what seems to be an inevitable conclusion that the most likely scenario for South Asia is that it will remain locked in an unstable situation. Their argument is that given the Indo-centric nature of the region, any change will require that India becomes more accommodating, but that India may regard accommodation as unnecessary given that it considers itself powerful enough to cope with any tension in the subcontinent. Such reluctance will then serve to strengthen anti-Indian hawks in Pakistan and as a consequence economic cooperation will not develop in a proper way. The better way to handle the issue is to strengthen the economic cooperation and in this process this will spill over to other areas and eventually will lead to the greater integration of the region.

Opportunities for SAARC

Conducive Environment for Cooperation

Being the biggest and most influential member nation, India must appreciate that by its not taking the lead, the SAARC will never achieve its full potential. India also needs to recognise the benefits of maintaining good relations with its neighbours and resolving contentious issues with them. The Indian government needs to display magnanimity, without compromising its national interests to settle all issues with its neighbours on terms that smaller nations will find attractive.[65] India needs to take positive steps to change the hegemonic attitude it is seen as having in the region. In order to remove deep-rooted mistrust, smaller nations will also need to play their part in the resolution of all contentious issues, thereby bringing stability in the region.

India and Pakistan should seek to resolve their differences, if the SAARC is to be effective and progressive.[66] Smaller nations must be accommodative of India's regional and global aspirations,[67] and they must view India as an opportunity for economic growth and development of their human resource capabilities, in particular in the field of information technology.[68] Improving bilateral relations with China may be acceptable to India. However, any attempt to balance or reduce Indian influence in the region will not be welcomed by India. An environment free of mutual mistrust and suspicion, conducive to cooperation and with India as leading member, would help the SAARC to grow and achieve the aims as mentioned in the charter for which it was created.

Sub-regional Approach

Working towards sub-regional cooperation on common themes will help to develop harmonious relations among member states, thus helping the SAARC to realise its true potential.[69] Steps to physically integrate the region will help to increase trade and improve economic relations, which besides increasing regional inter-dependence and bringing prosperity to the sub-region, underscores the importance of stability and resolution of inter-state disputes.[70] Efforts to create social linkages at sub-regional level in the fields of education, poverty alleviation, health, science, technology and tourism will bring direct benefits to the populace, thus spreading the SAARC awareness and strengthening the organisation.[71] Eric Gonsalves a former Secretary in the Government of India has said, that 'in South Asia almost no effort is devoted to advertising the genuine benefits that would accrue to every citizen from regionalisation, this needs to be remedied.'[72] The importance of communicating the potential benefits of SAARC, within and outside the region, cannot be overstated.

International Image

By improving inter-state relations and adopting a multilateral approach, SAARC can project itself as a united entity, thus improving its international image. Active engagement with the observer countries will attract foreign investment and other support which will boost development within the region.[73] India having established itself in the world, should take the lead in showcasing the SAARC achievements while engaging with the West. Initiatives such as laying a network of gas pipelines in the region can help project the SAARC as the 'Asian Gas Grid',[74] thus promoting itself as a useful organisation.[75]

Greater interaction with ASEAN[76] and the adoption of relevant lessons from its success will go a long way in helping SAARC's cause and put it on the path of progress.[77] The future of SAARC is tied up with the containment of superpower activity in South Asia and the success or failure of that effort depends on the climate of security that can be established within the region. The establishment of a climate of security, in turn, depends on the Indian role in the region and the response of the smaller states. The presence of superpowers in a region usually undermines sovereignty while regional organisations are supposed to reinforce it. South Asia in the eighties was in the forefront of Soviet-American relations. The urgency for concerted action by the SAARC countries to prevail upon the superpowers to keep their conflicts outside the region cannot be overstated. General Zia-Ul-Haq referred to this kind of possibility in his statement that, our success in this endeavour (SAARC) could serve to inhibit great power rivalry and restrain their action in South Asia and the adjacent regions of the world.[78] But this does not seem to be happening. Superpower activity is on the increase in South Asia and SAARC appears to be quite helpless to put a stop to it. Only a fairly radical transformation in the present cautious approach of SAARC can bring about a change in the situation.

The conditions that need to be created are the climate of suspicion and distrust will have to be replaced by a sense of oneness based on the struggle for a better life. The variety of cultures and languages in South Asia does not take away from the unity of experience of all groups with exploitation, poverty, disease and neglect. The region must focus more on the unity of experiences rather than the differences. South Asians must learn to distinguish between technology for peace and technology that spreads hunger and death. Nuclear weapons in particular and armament in general must be discouraged so that the region can have a greater sense of security from the threat of a nuclear holocaust and save the resources that are being wasted on armament. South Asian newspapers and media must be encouraged not to promote the climate of misperception and negative images of one ethnic or religious group against another.

A positive role can be played by the media in promoting the philosophy of SAARC so that the people of the various states become more receptive to the tasks of regional cooperation. Economic cooperation that benefits all the states of the region equally is essential for self-reliance. Water and power resources, food and technology properly shared can change the destiny of many regions of South Asia which suffer from one shortage or another. Together, South Asian states have a large enough domestic market to absorb goods and services at a level with which few regions can compete. If conditions of security, economic well being and trust can be created within South Asia, SAARC can play an important role in limiting the involvement of the superpowers in the region. These conditions will make possible such bold steps as putting bilateral differences on the agenda of SAARC instead of seeking help from a superpower use of economic and other sanctions by the community against members who threaten or resort to the use of force. There need to be taken collective actions to deal with threats from outside the region such as the Sino-Indian conflict or the Afghanistan situation and agreement on a basic line of action vis-à-vis the superpowers. In the past South Asian states have relied a great deal on the super-powers, it is time they boldly test their ability to rely on each other.

India and Pakistan

The pre-partition ideological conflict is still a major determinant of relations between India and Pakistan. The two states went to war over Kashmir after a few weeks of partition, following Pakistan's rejection of Kashmir's accession to India. This war lasted for well over a year and set the tone of Indo-Pakistan relations for the years to come. The war was renewed in 1965 and 1971. Such hostile relations led to an arms race between them and prepared the ground for extra regional powers to meddle in the region's affairs. Pakistan joined the American-sponsored military alliances, SEATO (South East Asian Treaty Organisation) and CENTO (Central Treaty Organisation) through which it procured U.S. $1.3 billion worth of arms, logistics and training.[79] India diverted considerable resources to purchase and develop arms and armament technology from diverse sources. Thus, the subcontinent became a hot bed of cold war. The Indo-Pakistan War of 1971 and the subsequent emergence of Bangladesh as an independent entity brought about a basic change in the South Asian power equation. The power of Pakistan was substantially reduced. The Shimla Agreement of July 1972 provided a constructive basis for the normalisation of relations between the two countries it also provided for the restoration of travel and communication links. By 1975, both countries resumed the trade relations that had stopped following the 1965 war.

The restoration of the railway link between Lahore and Amritsar facilitated the exchange of goods between the two countries on an ad hoc basis. Both sides have shown interest in making long-term trade arrangements or are interested in limited industrial cooperation. A significant change in Pakistan's world outlook was evident in 1979 when it withdrew from SEATO and sought membership in the nonaligned movement. India readily recognised Pakistan's changed world outlook and promptly supported the latter's membership in the movement. However, a new complication arose following the Soviet intervention in Afghanistan. President Zia Ul-Haq's obsession with the threat to Pakistan's security and his search for external sources alarmed India. America's rearming of Pakistan with forty very sophisticated F-16 fighter bombers and the prediction that Pakistan would have a nuclear weapons capacity and an "Islamic bomb" by the mid-1980s concerned Indians very much, and some Indian ruling party leaders were known to have contemplated a preemptive military strike at Pakistan before the latter attained the capacity to launch a war against India.

Despite this hawkish talk, India is not likely to undertake such an adventure for three important reasons:

(1) The Indian economy is vulnerable to sanctions from Western-dominated financial institutions;

(2) Islamic states of West Asia, which supply almost one-third of India's oil imports, are likely to react very strongly against any attacks on Pakistan; and

(3) The Muslim minority community in India would have not supported an India-led war with Pakistan in the 1980's it did in the 1971 war that created Bangladesh.

In the light of such considerations, there is still the possibility of an accommodation with Pakistan on mutually acceptable terms. President Zia's 1981 endorsement of a no-war pact with India (which was originally proposed by Nehru in 1949), raised the Indo-Pakistani dialogue on security issues to a new level. Pakistan has indicated its interest in continuing this dialogue, and India has responded tentatively but positively.[80]

Notes

1. Bhatnagar, Stuti (2008), Interstate Conflicts and Regionalism in South Asia: Prospectus and Challenges, *Spring,* Summer, pp. 5-6.
2. John A.K. Bailes, et al (2007). 'Regionalism and Security Building', *Regionalism in South Asian Diplomacy,* SIPRI Policy Paper No. 15, Stockholm International Peace Research Institute, Sweden, p. 3.

3. Rahman, Atiur (2004), 'SAARC: Not yet a Community', *the Asia-Pacific: A Region in Transition,* ed. Jim Rolfe' *Asia-Pacific Center for Security Studies*, Honolulu, p.135.
4. Banerjee, Dipankar, (2002), "*SAARC in the Twenty-First Century: Towards a Cooperative Future*", India Research Press, New Delhi, pp.130-31.
5. Mukherji, I.N.(2002), "*South Asian Preferential Trading Agreement: An Assessment of its Impact*", in SAARC in the Twenty-First Century, New Delhi, p.114.
6. Chibber, Bharti (2004), *"Regional Security and Regional Cooperation: A Comparative Study of ASEAN and SAARC",* New Century Publications, New Delhi, p. 96.
7. Rajan, K.V. (2011), 'Renewing SAARC', *Institute of Foreign Affairs, Nepal,* p. 1.
8. Bhasin, Madhav (2008), "India's Role in South Asia – Perceived Hegemony or Reluctant Leadership, *Indian Foreign Affairs*, *globalindiafoundation,* Vol. 3, no. 4, p.7.
9. The World Factbook', *Central Intelligence Agency,* retrieved 05 May 2011,<https://www.cia.gov/library/publications/the-world-factbook/rankorder/2001rank.html>.
10. Sridharan, Kripa (2008), 'Regional Organisations and Conflict Management: Comparing ASEAN and SAARC', *Crisis States Research Centre,* Working Paper Series, Vol. 2, No. 33, March 20, pp. 1-30.
11. Chaturvedy, Rajeev Ranjan and Malone, David M (2009), 'India and its South Asian Neighbours', *Institute of South Asian Studies, National University of Singapore (NUS),* Working Paper No. 100, 26. pp. 1-37.
12. Sabur, A.K.M. Abdus and Kabir, Mohammad Humayun (2000), *Conflict Management and Sub Regional Co-operation in ASEAN: Relevance for SAARC,* Academic Press and Publishers Limited in association with Bangladesh Institute of International and Strategic Studies, Dhaka, 2000, pp.74-76.
13. *Ibid*. 53.
14. Pattanaik, Smruti S (2004), 'Indo-Pak Relations and the SAARC Summits', *Strategic Analysis, Institute for Defence Studies and Analyses,* Vol. 28, no. 3, p. 429.
15. Chibber, Bharti (2004), *Regional Security and Regional Cooperation: A Comparative Study of ASEAN and SAARC,* New Century Publications, New Delhi, pp. 301-302.
16. Snedden, Christopher (2010), 'Some thoughts about the South Asian region' East Asia Forum.
17. *Ibid.*
18. Rajan, K.V. (2011), 'Renewing SAARC', *Institute of Foreign Affairs, Nepal*, p. 1.

19. Poorna, Rodrigo (2010), 'Analysis & Opinion: President Nasheed's no nonsense SAARC speech', *Asian Tribune*.
20. Snedden, Christopher (2010), "Some thoughts about the South Asian region" East Asia Forum.
21. Murthy, Padmaja (2000), 'Relevance of SAARC', *Strategic Analysis, Institute for Defence Studies and Analyses,* Vol. 23, No. 10, p. 2.
22. Pattanaik, Smruti S (2006), 'Making Sense of Regional Cooperation: SAARC at Twenty', *Strategic Analysis, Institute for Defence Studies and Analyses*, Vol. 30, No. 1, p. 155.
23. Lama, Mahindra P (2008), 'Monitoring of SAARC Policies and Programmes, *Centre for Policy and Analysis Studies,* Islamabad. p. 6.
24. K. Khatri, Sridhar and W. Kueck (2003), *"Terrorism in South Asia: Impacts on Development and Democratic Process"* RCSS (Colombo), Konrad Adenauer Foundation (New Delhi) and Shipra Publications (Delhi), pp. 23-24.
25. *Ibid*. p. 672.
26. *Ibid*. p. 673.
27. Pattanaik Smruti S. (2010), 'Time to Redeem SAARC', *Institute for Defence Studies and Analyses*. New Delhi, p. 5-6.
28. Raj, Nayar Baldev (1977), "United States and India: New Directions and Their Context, *Economic and Political Weekly*, Vol.12, no.45-46, p.1906.
29. Jaffrelot, Christopher (2009), "The India-US Rapprochement: State-driven or Middle Class-driven", *India Quarterly*, A Journal of International Studies, Vol. 65, No. 1, New Delhi pp. 5-8.
30. World Bank, south Asian region: towards a climate change strategy, URL; www.indianenvironmentportal.org.in/content/towards-a-climate-change-strategy-south-asia-region.
31. United Nations framework convention on climate change (UNFCCC), Which defines "climate change as a change of climate which is attributed directly or indirectly to human activity that alters the composition of the global atmosphere and which is in addition to natural climate variability observed over comparable time periods."
32. Sharma, Suman (2012), "Environmental Issues and SAARC Initiatives," *World Focus*, New Delhi, p.14.
33. United Nations Framework Convention on Climate Change.
34. SAARC Workshop: Climate Change and Disasters-Emerging Trends and Future Strategies, 20-21 August 2008, Kathmandu, Nepal, SAARC Disasters Management Centre New Delhi.
35. Ghosh, Shubham (2012), *"Look around Policy Key to SAARC's Future",* One India News, p. 1.

36. Kumar, Vikas (2011), "Why is SAARC gridlock and how can it be revitalised", East Asia Forum Economics, Politics and Public Policy in East Asia and the Pacific, http://www.eastasiaforum.org
37. Bhanot, Monica (1999); "Challenges to Regional Cooperation in South Asia: A New Perspective" *Online Journal of Peace and Conflict* at http:// www.trinstitute.org/ojpcr/toc2 3.htm, August 2-3. pp. 2-3.
38. Chaturvedy, Rajeev Ranjan (2007): "*Democracy in Nepal: Issues and Challenges*, SSPC (Society for the Study of Peace and Conflict Studies), New Delhi, pp. 1-2.
39. The political debate is primarily centered on the issue of Tamil separatist movement and Sinhalese (two ethnic groups of Sri Lanka). The ethnic issues have pushed Sri Lanka into the brink of civil war for nearly twenty years, which has not yet been solved despite the international mediation.
40. Bhatnagar, Stuti (2008), Interstate Conflicts and Regionalism in South Asia: Prospectus and Challenges, *Spring,* Summer, pp. 5-6.
41. Haider, Zaglul, (2001), "Crises of Regional Cooperation in South Asia," *Security Dialogue*, Sage Publications, Vol.32 n.4, New Delhi, p. 427.
42. The Treaty of Peace and Friendship between India and Nepal is a major point of debate between India and Nepal as it completely ignores Nepal's right to decide anything on its own sphere.
43. Nepal fell under the grip of Maoist movement in 1996 and since then more than 10000 people have been killed in the insurgency.
44. Kaushik, Mahan and Rampant (1991), *India and South Asia*, South Asian Publishers, New Delhi, pp. 24-25.
45. The main point of debate hinges on the Charter of SAARC which does not allow bilateral issues to be discussed at the regional level summit diplomacy.
46. Murty, S. (1993), *"The Changing Indian Economic Order*", Indus Publications, New Delhi, p. 151.
47. The Charter of the SAARC does not allow to discuss bilateral and contentious issues but it's always because of these issues SAARC Summits have been interrupted and failed to evolve as a true bloc. It seems that SAARC should consider bilateral and contentious issues to be discussed for its long life.
48. Carrot and stick theory has been the main mantra of Indian cooperation in the region.
49. Zaki Ibrahim Hussain (1994), 'Recent Developments in SAARC and Prospects for the future', *South Asian Survey*, New Delhi, p. 2.
50. The 11th Summit was interrupted because of military coup in Pakistan and hijacking of Indian airlines plane from Kathmandu. Due to attack in the Indian parliament in 2002 by the Islamic militant, which India considers Pakistan behind the scene?

51. Lodhi, Maheela (2001), *"Viewpoint: Security Challenges in South Asia the Non-proliferation Review"*, summer, p. 118.
52. Bhanot, Monica (1999), "Challenges to Regional Cooperation in South Asia: A New Perspective' Online Journal of Peace and Conflict at http://www.trinstitute.org/ojpcr/toc2 3.htm.
53. *Ibid.*
54. *Ibid.*
55. Religious tensions between Hindus and Muslims in India have sparked off infamous violence in the state of Gujarat, India in 2002 where approximately more than 2000 persons were killed.
56. Srinivasan et al. (1995): *South Asian Economic Development: Trade and Economic Development*, p. 147.
57. *Ibid.* p. 147.
58. Dawn, September 22, 1987, and the Muslim, October 22, 1987.
59. Sikkim used to be a small state in Northeastern part of India, which was ceded into it by force.
60. I K Gujral first became India's foreign minister and then Prime Minister in mid 1990s and he enunciated Gujral Doctrine.
61. Murthy, Padma (1999), "The Gujral Doctrine and Beyond", Strategic Analysis; *A monthly Journal of the IDSA*, Vol. XXIII. No. 4, New Delhi, p. 17.
62. Under SAPTA, SAARC countries have agreed on tariff provisions only on 226 objects.
63. Ghanshyam, N. Singh (1993), "*The Economy of the SAARC Nations*", Anmol Publications, New Delhi, pp. 125-126.
64. Prime Minister Rajiv Gandhi has made the announcement that India is reconsidering the decision to not build nuclear weapons.
65. Ram, Amar Nath (2009), 'SAARC in a Globalised Era – Imperatives and Opportunities', *India Quarterly: A Journal of International Affairs,* Vol. 65, No. 4, p. 444.
66. Pandian, S.G. (2002), 'Moving South Asia's economies beyond the Indo-Pakistan paradigm in the South Asian Regional Association for Cooperation', *Contemporary South Asia,* Vol. 11, No. 3, p. 342.
67. Sabur, A.K.M. Abdus and Kabir, Mohammad Humayun (2000), *Conflict Management and Sub Regional Co-operation in ASEAN: Relevance for SAARC,* Academic Press and Publishers Limited in association with Bangladesh Institute of International and Strategic Studies, Dhaka, p. 93.
68. Rajan, K.V. (2011), 'Renewing SAARC', *Institute of Foreign Affairs, Nepal*, p. 5.

69. Pattnaik, Smruti S (2006), 'Making Sense of Regional Cooperation: SAARC at Twenty', *Strategic Analysis (Institute for Defence Studies and Analyses),* Vol. 30, no. 1, p. 156.
70. Sabur, AK.M. Abdus and Kabir, Mohammad Humayun (2000), *Conflict Management and Sub Regional Co-operation in ASEAN: Relevance for SAARC,* Academic Press and Publishers Limited in association with Bangladesh Institute of International and Strategic Studies, p. 168.
71. Ram, Amar Nath (2009), 'SAARC in a Globalised Era – Imperatives and Opportunities', *India Quarterly: A Journal of International Affairs,* Vol. 65, no. 4, p. 445.
72. Chibber, Bharti (2004), *Regional Security and Regional Cooperation: A Comparative Study of ASEAN and SAARC,* New Century Publications, New Delhi, p. 215.
73. Mavara, Inayat (2007), 'The South Asian Association for Regional Cooperation', *Stockholm International Peace Research Institute (SIPRI),* Policy Paper no. 15, p. 24.
74. South Asia has common borders, on one side, with Central and West Asia, major energy producing regions, and on the other, with South East Asia and China, major energy consumers.
75. Rajan, K.V. (2011), 'Renewing SAARC', *Institute of Foreign Affairs, Nepal,* p. 4.
76. ASEAN: An Association of South East Asian Nations formed in 1967 Through Bangkok Treaty.
77. Chibber, Bharti (2004), *Regional Security and Regional Cooperation: A Comparative Study of ASEAN and SAARC,* New Century Publications, New Delhi. pp. 214-215.
78. Jabeen, Musrat and et.al (2010), SAARC and Indo-Pak relationship, *Journal of Political Studies*, vol. 1, issues 2, pp. 127-145.
79. Cohen, Stephen P. (1976), "U.S. Weapons and South Asia: A Policy Analysis," *Pacific Affairs*, Vol. 49, No.1, spring, p. 50.
80. *Ibid.*

Chapter - 5

Conclusion

The creation of regional organisations has become an order and necessity at the international fora in post world war II period. The post-colonial phase in international relations has witnessed a distinct trend towards regional unity. With the growing strength of this trend, a large number of states from different states of the world constitute themselves into regional groupings to give fresh impetus to a wide variety of cooperative ventures based on the given region. Regionalism in general has proved to be a collective device to serve economic, political and social objectives of those states. The proliferation of diverse regional organisations like the European Union (EU), Association of South East Asian Nations (ASEAN), Asia Pacific Economic Cooperation (APEC) etc. offer adequate evidence of this proposition. As a viable response in a rapidly globalised world, the trend towards regionalism is being espoused by both developed as well as developing countries. The people of South Asian region are also attempting to share their experiences in addressing their common problems through a South Asian Association of Regional Cooperation (SAARC). The eight nations that comprise SAARC are Afghanistan, Bangladesh, Bhutan, India, Maldives, Nepal, Pakistan and Sri Lanka are bounded by geographical contiguity; common culture, ethnic and religious ties, but is plagued by political differences that come in the way of speedy developments of SAARC and the countries that comprise it. SAARC consequently could not score a success as other economic groupings (EU, ASEAN, NAFTA and MERCOSAR) even after 26 years of its existence. However, this is not to underrate some of its role in other areas of mutual cooperation.

The South Asian countries are having various common economic problems like poverty, income inequality, large population dependence on agriculture, low productivity, mass unemployment and industrial backwardness which further adds to the already existing underdevelopment and unemployment in this region.

To overcome these socio-economic problems, the South Asian association of regional cooperation was launched with vigour from the member countries although with some reservations and initial hiccups from some of its members. The idea of regional cooperation in South Asia was first initiated by President of Bangladesh late Zia Ur Rehman, who visited India, Nepal, Pakistan and Sri Lanka during the period of 1977-1980 to explore the possibilities of regional cooperation among the South Asian countries. In May 1980, he issued a formal call for SAARC regional cooperation. His call received a positive response from all the countries except two major powers of South Asia, India and Pakistan who were initially hesitant to form the regional organisation but later on they too accepted the idea. Hence the consultation at official level was carried out for the proposed cooperation. These preliminary exchanges at different levels i.e., foreign secretaries and foreign ministers clearly brought out that the proposed cooperation should on the one hand, reflect the spirit of mutual trust, understanding and sympathetic appreciation of political inspiration existing among the countries of the region and on the principles of sovereign equality, territorial integrity and non-interference in internal affairs of each other. The first ever regional summit of the heads of the states or governments of seven SAARC countries was held in Dhaka (Bangladesh) on December 7, 1985 after about four and a half years preparation. Contentious and bilateral politico-security issues were deliberately kept outside the purview of SAARC.

Since the establishment of SAARC 17 summits were held in its twenty five years of existence: Dhaka-1985, Bangalore 1986, Kathmandu 1987, Islamabad 1988, Male 1990, Colombo 1991, Dhaka 1993, New Delhi 1995, Male 1997, Colombo 1998, Kathmandu 2002, Islamabad 2004, New Delhi 2007, Colombo 2008, Thimpu 2010, Addu city Male 2011.

Some of the notable achievements of SAARC are:

The establishment of the SAARC food security reserve- meant to meet emergency situations in the region.

- The agreement and ratification of the SAARC regional convention on suppression of terrorism.
- The agreement on the SAARC regional convention on narcotic drugs and psychotropic substances.
- The formulation of a procedure for projection of SAARC collective positions at international fora.
- The establishment of SAARC University at Delhi.

The focusing of activity on selected important social issues, such as poverty alleviation, child survival and rights of the child, status youth and their integration in national development, exploitation of the girl child, women in development, needs of disabled persons, shelter and housing, eradication of illiteracy, drug trafficking and drug abuse, integration of demographic objectives and control of population strategies in national development plans.

The establishment of networking agreements in some of the fields in science and technology (biotechnology, genetic engineering, energy modeling techniques etc.) the setting up in 1991 of the SARC fund for regional project (SERP) which will now be merged with the SAARC regional fund to form the South Asian development fund (SADF) to mobilise global surplus for the development of the SAARC region.

The framing of guidelines and procedures for granting recognition by SAARC to regional apex bodies with a view to ensuring great participation of the non-governmental organisations (NGO's) including professional bodies in the private sector, in the process of promoting socio-economic and cultural development of South Asia as envisaged in the SAARC charter. Recognition has already been accorded to the SAARC chamber of commerce and industry SCCI and SAARC-LAW as association for persons of the legal communities of SAARC countries.

The formation of the association of SAARC speakers and parliamentarians

The most important achievement of SAARC was agreement establishing South Asian preferential trade agreement (SAPTA) which now is moving to South Asia free trade area in 2006.

This agreement would go a long way in achieving the basic objectives of SAARC.

Besides the above mentioned achievements of SAARC, the working procedure has made it possible for the member countries to hold regular meetings at various levels and offered opportunities for the exchange of views in non-controversial areas of cooperation. As an offshoot of the regular encounters, the meetings have also facilitated behind the scene consultations among the regional leaders which have frequently produced positive results.

Despite some positive developments, SAARC is still very far from maturing as a regional grouping. Its scope of cooperation did not extended to hardcore economic areas for almost eight years after its establishment. It took another two years to launch the first economic area in the form of SAARC preferential trading arrangement (SAPTA) and ten years in order to move from SAPTA (South Asia Preferential Trading Arrangement) to SAFTA (South Asian Free Trade Area) in 2006. Consequently the SAARC countries have not developed any collective leverage in global economic forums. This is apart from the continuing costs that the member states are incurring due to non-cooperation in these areas. There are still economic areas, like energy, manufacturing, services, money and finance which are still outside the purview of SAARC cooperation. On the whole the association has made very little headway in realising its primary objectives to promote the welfare of the people of South Asia and to improve their quality of life.

Even in the areas where SAARC has been active over the last two decades or so, several of the decisions taken at the highest political level remain unimplemented. The impact of the activities carried out under the integrated programme of action has suffered due to adhoc selection of such activities, their short-term nature, delineated set of priorities for the selection of such activities and plans of action to implement them. Besides, representation in the meetings organised under the IPA has been at relatively low levels and problems have been encountered in the follow up and implementation. Conspicuous failure of the IPA (Integrated programme of action) has been its inability to generate and implement regional programmes for harnessing complementarities within the region, as originally envisaged in the SAARC charter. None of the four regional centres have emerged as a recognised centre of excellence in the region. They have been bogged down by routine activities and are hardly distinguishable from the central centre with which they are associated. The facilities provided under the SAARC food security reserve had never been utilised, even though member states have suffered from acute food shortage from time to time. The two conventions on suppression of terrorism and narcotics drugs and psychotropic substances have had no impact on controlling terrorism or drug trafficking through regional cooperation in South Asia. The schemes of people to people contact have been stagnating at their existing levels and have degenerated into a mere tokenism. A vast number of people in South Asia still encounter formidable difficulties in moving from one country to another and getting access to information regarding other countries on the pretext of security and other political considerations. In the field of environment, SAARC has made no progress beyond producing some studies. This is all the more regrettable because the cost of non-cooperation in this area is colossal. So far SAARC has achieved a limited success. The reason why it has not been able to garner greater success like other regional organisation like European Union (EU) and Association of South East Asian Nations ASEAN is the hard and painful fact that bilateral differences between member states continue to cast long shadows on the prospects of meaningful cooperation. These differences are basically political in nature and include internal political tensions affecting interstate relations, bilateral disputes and differences; and conflicting external perceptions and security alignments. On the top of these domestic problems lies a layer of local, unresolved interstate disputes and conflicts which continue to cast a long shadow on the prospects of regional cooperation. On the top of these interstate disputes is the dispute between the two superpowers of the region India and Pakistan which is considered the single most obstacles in the process of regional cooperation. In fact, it is this conflictual relationship between these two big countries that have hampered the SAARC progress.

India and Pakistan the two biggest neighbouring countries of South Asia have much in common in terms of history, culture, language and religion. Both the countries were parts of a single political entity until mid-August 1947. Despite these close affinities psychologically both the countries have always been living two poles apart. When British left the sub-continent, it was widely expected that the geographical location, historical connections, socio-cultural, commonalities, ethnic and linguistic affinities of the two countries would pave a way for peace for the entire region, but the reality has turned out to be different. Since their independence both the countries have grown ever further apart and their policies both the domestic and international have evolved increasingly in divergent directions. During near six decades of their existence, the two countries have fought three full-fledged conventional wars and several small border skirmishes and thus their relations remained by and large deteriorated most of the time.

Among all other major factors, the Kashmir issue remained the most dominant factor of India and Pakistan relations, bringing them twice to the brink of war. It has been an outstanding security preoccupation as much to Pakistan as to India, an actual and potential destabiliser of the entire geostrategic balance of the subcontinent.

Right from SAARC's inception both India and Pakistan had their reservations regarding its aims, objectives and working. When the idea of SAARC was proposed by Bangladesh both India and Pakistan were initially skeptical. India was suspicious of a western hand behind the idea. It was also apprehensive that the organisation perhaps would provide a forum for India bashing and ganging up its neighbours. Similarly Pakistan too was apprehensive, its initial reluctance to join SAARC was partly conditioned by its apprehensions about the organisation being harnessed by India to further its hegemonic design in the region and it did not want its efforts of forging closer ties with West Asian countries to be hampered by joining SAARC.

Finally, both India and Pakistan decided to join the SAARC due to their own reasons. In the political context, India could not afford the risk of isolating itself regionally from the grouping of the states that could also include Pakistan. However, it insisted that all bilateral and conflictual issues should be kept outside the SAARC framework. Pakistan too decided to join the SAARC forum because it wanted to be an active member of the region with full participation. It also felt that by working with other small members of SAARC, it could counter the Indian ambition to dominate the region.

Regarding India's hegemonistic ambitions it is understandable that India being the largest country in the region expects to be regarded as the leader of the South Asian group not only in the SAARC but in other international forums as well, including the Non-Aligned Movement. However, to be acceptable in such a role, India would have to adopt a more generous and responsible attitude and shed animosities towards its smaller neighbours. It must also "develop such a political and moral equation which infuses confidence" leading to harmony and mutual trust. It must muster the support of Pakistan as well as all other countries open heartedly for the betterment and prosperity of the entire group. To remove the aura of mistrust and psychological barrier to detente India maintaining her pivotal role could adopt a more conciliatory attitude towards all the member states particularly neighbours with common borders. This attitude will not tilt the balance against India in any field but would instead create an atmosphere of confidence, which would promote cooperation without challenging India's leverage in the region. The author emphasises that the most important and primary objective before SAARC is to make genuine progress towards the creation of good-will and understanding amongst member states. This would in turn lead to "the process of enhancement of overall stability" and bear positive results in economic, social, scientific and other fields. Pointing out some major factors which hinder the path of regional integration in the South Asian region, this is to suggested that (a) disparate levels of industrialisation and resource endowment (b) varying sizes of internal markets (c) different political orientation of the countries belonging to the region (d) ideological differences. Therefore, it would be advisable to continue the efforts towards 'regional cooperation' in the economic field rather than attempting to develop interdependence of 'regional integration till such time that an atmosphere of mutual goodwill and trust is established among the participants of SAARC. A very important and useful feature of this book is the profuseness of tables and charts providing data ranging from comparisons of armed forces of SAARC countries, the external military assistance received by these countries, to figures on intra-regional trade and country-wise economy indicating.

To keep SAARC on track and to achieve its objectives of socio-economic development and as a precondition for joining the organisation by India, bilateral and contentious issues were kept out of its ambit.

India and Pakistan are having two divergent views regarding the bilateral issues and SAARC. India views SAARC as an organisation for social, cultural and economic development and it should not take up bilateral issues which are political in nature. India supported its view on the basis of that various political problems that have existed between the member states have a long history of misunderstanding and, therefore, to burden SAARC with resolving them will not hamper the process of regional cooperation but also inhibit the organisations socio-economic agenda. On the other hand, Pakistan supports the other view that bilateral contentious issues are the basis hurdles in establishing mutual trust among SAARC countries. Pakistan's position in this regard has been resolution of all territorial disputes could give fresh impetus to SAARC, if we want to move forward we must resolve and remove all territorial disputes, says Pakistan.

SAARC's failure to take up bilateral political issues has been attributed as one of the major reasons for the failure of regional cooperation. Most of the smaller countries having larger economic interests and greater expectations from regional cooperation have attributed the lack of progress in the SAARC to the existence of conflictual bilateral relations between India and Pakistan. The pressure to include bilateral and contentious issues in SAARC deliberations increased with the passage of time. It is being suggested that on the sidelines of every SAARC summit there is a meeting of foreign ministers of India and Pakistan to settle their bilateral issues. Bilateral issues became reason for the postponement of summit meetings e.g.,

1992, 1999, 2001, and 2003 etc. almost in every summit these bilateral issues created a lot of mistrust and misunderstanding among the participating countries. These issues have been the formidable barriers to the growth of SAARC. Hitherto, it is realised that SAARC may not achieve its desired goals without harmonising the bilateral irritants.

Collective economic benefits have been the main rationale as well as the drive behind SAARC's creation. However, the performance of SAARC has been far from encouraging. After 25 years of its inception, it is yet to evolve in to a structural trading block enough to generate intense economic activity among its member countries. Although the member countries finalised two framework agreements on SAPTA in 1993 and SAFTA in 2004 with the hope that these would help in increasing trade between the member countries. The intraregional trade in South Asia continues to constitute only four per cent of the total regions overall trade as against European Union's 72 per cent and ASEAN 22 per cent.

India and Pakistan who accounts 80 per cent of SAARC's gross domestic product, their contribution to intra-SAARC trade is very low. The legal trade between the two countries has been very small and in the last decade has varied between a low of US$ 106 million in 1994-95 to a high of US $ 321 million in 1998-99. This shows clearly the volume and scale of trade between the two countries has been very small in absolute terms and as a percentage of the total trade of both countries.

Efforts to reduce the economic asymmetry of SAARCs member states have suffered because of their mutual political mistrust stemming from both uncertainties as to the organisations aims as well as bilateral disputer. This is particularly true in the case of India and Pakistan. Pakistan argues that full scale economic cooperation in the region cannot be brought in an environment of tension and conflict. In an indirect reference to its long standing dispute with India over Jammu and Kashmir, Pakistan maintain that multilateral trade regimes in SAARC regime cannot function in a political vacuum, and the resolution of bilateral issues with India must come first. However,

India opposed this view, sighting SAARC's primary objectives is to exclude bilateral contentious issues.

The failure to create better trade relations between India and Pakistan has forced these two states to look for alternative distant supply sources and thus depriving them of the potential to exploit economies of scale and their associated caste reduction effects. The potential for bilateral trade between India and Pakistan is enormous and cooperation would be beneficial to both the countries. Hence the failure story of SAARC in the economic field may be directly attributed to the hostile relations between India and Pakistan.

Terrorism has been one of the most burning issues which have created a lot of mistrust among the SAARC countries. It has been one of the vital issues which are responsible for the low performance of SAARC. While almost all the SAARC countries except the Maldives are facing the problem of terrorism, the political agenda of all these countries are extremely diverse and often in sharp contrast with regard to the issue of terrorism. In the context of India and Pakistan this issue has created a lot of mistrust and misunderstanding between the two countries. India brands Kashmiri separatist movement as Pakistan sponsored terrorist activities but Pakistan always maintained that the Kashmiri struggle is legitimate freedom struggle and made every effort to have a clear distinction between freedom struggle and terrorism. SAARC has ratified three regional conventions (1987, 1997, and 2004) on suppression of terrorism, which provides for exchange of information, intelligences and expertise to combat terrorism. But it has achieved little success in the South Asian context; the member states have accused each other country. If terrorists of one country where adjudged as freedom fighters in another country and vice versa, then this problem will always cast its shadow on the future of SAARC.

If the conflictual relations of South Asian countries in general and the hostile environment of India and Pakistan in particular has undetermined the working and performance of SAARC, but in return to it this organisation has provided a suitable meeting ground where the leaders of South Asian countries especially of India and Pakistan meet and discuss bilateral problems informally. This organisation has been playing an important role, albeit an indirect one, in promoting regional peace by defusing the bilateral tensions. It has done so by providing an informal avenue where leaders of the two countries could meet on regular basis to discuss and address bilateral and even multilateral differences. Thereby reducing the chances of conflict and leading to greater understanding. The importance of the SAARC forums lies in the fact that these meetings are regular informal, hence regional leaders can meet without domestic repercussions even at times of acute bilateral tensions. In the past various summit meetings on the sidelines of SAARC; these meetings helped to diffuse the tensions and paved the way for talks. The Indo-Pak relations have been benefitted time and again from these informal meetings.

From the above discussion, it becomes clear that in South Asia the two main protagonists are India and Pakistan. When these two countries are at peace with each other, South Asia is by and large are at peace. If they have troubled relations, South Asia is uneasy. When these two nations fight, South Asia trembles. India and Pakistan as the main powers of the region determine in their war and peace, the present and future of South Asia.

Besides the Indo-Pakistan hostility there are other several major impediments which are also responsible for the slow process of SAARC. First, the vast imbalance between India and all its neighbours, especially the concerns of least developed countries (LDCs) about both insecurity and economic vulnerability. It had to be a positive symmetry, as pursued by former Prime Minister of India, I.K. Gujral, since there could not be symmetry between opposite poles of the scale. But this was not followed up, leaving LDCs (least developed countries) with a plethora of complains.

Second, India felt it more convenient to take the bilateral route in its relation with its neighbours. Instead of becoming an anchorship for the regional grouping that demanded an accommodation of smaller neighbour concerns.

Third, the current structure of SAARC and its central secretariat cannot cope with such a big agenda that requires an efficient body and expertise on merit, rather than on the basis of quota for lethargic bureaucrats from foreign ministers on a rotational procedure. The SAARC secretariat needs more authority and its secretary general needs to be a world class manager, a visionary of an economist rather than a bureaucrat.

Regional co-operation would have a greater chance of success if simple, workable goals rather than publicly pronounced grandiose, show-case items are set and carefully pursued, and if there is the indigenisation of plans, solutions and outcomes (that is, if members solve problems through discussion and consensus among themselves with minimal external interference). Once these basic priorities are set, the process towards a regional community would have begun. Another characteristic worth considering is the style of the decision-making process and negotiation. Informality, thorough discussion and consensus without coercion are the most effective procedure. It undoubtedly takes time for governments to come to understand one another and to be able to consult with each other regularly and informally instead of resorting to formal meetings and treaties. Similarly, it requires a slow, searching process to discover which issues would be acceptable for discussion and which would be offensive or antagonistic and are therefore to be avoided. Public exposure is also crucial in promoting co-operation; media and academic involvement are complementary to state interaction. ASEAN has been credited with easing tensions through a system of informality and frequent discussions. Problems arising within the grouping have also been, in large measure, kept in check as a result of consultation and dialogue at various levels of government machinery. These are some areas in which SAARC may want to follow suit. Neighbours and geography cannot change, India as a bigger country of the region has to demonstrate large heartedness.

This is the era of the generation the process now should be people-led rather than elite-led. Regional cooperation is the only answer to multifarious problems of the region. Baggage of history has to be overcome.

Lessons of EU, ASEAN and others to be imbibed seriously, Political will crucial. If trade does not cross-borders the armies will.

- Further Liberalisation of Visa regimes: the liberalisation of visa will enhance the people to people contact freely without the constraints of borders.

- Trade to Open Gradually for mutual benefits: The trade should be opened so that both the trading partners should get benefitted.
- Subaltern approach; bottom up rather than top down: living in the democratic era where the wellbeing of the downtrodden sections matters more than the upper sections of society the policies should be downtrodden rather than the upward.
- Joint Projects involving SAARC countries symbolising concrete cooperation (highways, dams, hospitals, Universities: The projects should be stated involving many countries so that both can enhance their energy.
- Media to be positive and highlight commonalities and strong features of the countries. The media should try to be positive. It should try to create the peaceful situation rather than destruct the already disturbed region.
- Smaller states should be allowed to benefit from the higher levels of development in the information technology sector in India.
- There is a need to expand trade and investment in the emerging global context to strengthen the regional economic bloc. Facilitating the free flow of financial and physical capital and also streamlining the movement of personnel in the region.
- Targeted uplifting of the production and export base of the weaker economies in the region; and
- Establishing a South Asian identify in terms of brand names, quality, standards, investment regimes and other areas where a common approach would be to the benefit of all.

Index

S

T